I0201746

This personal copy of

The Power of the Cross

Belongs to:

If found, please contact me at

Printed in the United States of America

ISBN-13: 978-0692266045 (Custom)
ISBN-10: 0692266046

FreedomHouse Publishing
12146 Millford Lane N
Jacksonville, FL 32246

www.freedomhousenow.com

FreedomMinistry International

Level One

The Power of Cross

INTRODUCTION

Welcome to FreedomMinistry! Let's begin a journey of discipling that will literally transform your life! Tens of thousands of people are already taking this journey along with you, and tens of thousands of testimonies confirm that its Biblical principles, when consistently and genuinely practiced, produce lasting life-change.

Whether you are experiencing FreedomMinistry Level 1 in a small group, seminar, five-day Intensive, or three-day Concentrate, anticipate ample opportunities to appropriate the power of the Cross to defeat your spiritual enemies, break cycles of unwanted behavior, and learn how to experience greater freedom both now and in the future.

You arrive at this seminar with spiritual issues. You may not have lived a day of your life without some of these issues. But, you will never be the same again! As you surrender these issues to the power of the Cross, you will experience real, spiritual freedom!

We have mapped this seminar out carefully, to bring you step-by-step into the freedom that full surrender releases into your life.

FORMATS AND VENUES

FreedomMinistry is easily adaptable to several group types and sizes. It functions in large venues of hundreds or thousands, yet operates just as powerfully and personally in small groups of 10 or 20.

FreedomMinistry meets in weekly ministry sessions preparatory to an IMPACT weekend of powerful personal ministry. Many group sizes, venues, and scheduling commitments are possible. In whatever setting you are experiencing Level 1, surrendering to the power of the Cross is your key to success.

The effectiveness of FreedomMinistry depends upon the leaders doing the ministry, the intercessors committed to prayer and fasting, and the level of personal surrender your strength of will allows. We have discovered that only committed intercessors and prepared leaders, who release the power of the Cross and through the work of Holy Spirit, can make the spiritual power required for change in your life available. This is not a program or a seminar that simply exposes you to information; it is a strategy of Holy Spirit to begin a life of spiritual restoration!

A Discipling Ministry

FreedomMinistry materials and methods are not magical, nor does personal transformation, as previously stated, derive simply from exposure to principles even when they are God's principles. In fact, experiencing FreedomMinistry as "research for ministry" really misses the spiritual emphasis altogether.

The personal, spiritual heart condition of the leaders receiving and releasing determines the effectiveness of discipling to bring people into redemptive restoration. And, FreedomMinistry is, above all things, a discipling ministry.

Jesus used a discipling model and method to prepare His leaders. He shared 'what He did' with His disciples so they could do 'what He did.' He promised this shared spiritual experience would prepare and position them to 'do greater than He did.'

Jesus discipled the leaders He commissioned to represent Him, the believers who would perpetuate what He established. Then, He told His leaders to disciple others.

Jesus' discipling model defines the mission of all believers. In the command that tells us what we are supposed to do as His representatives, Jesus gives one clear, over-arching imperative: "Wherever you go, disciple."

When they saw him, they worshipped him. Yet some held back, unsure. Jesus approached and charged them: "I have all authority in Heaven and earth (given to Me so I can give it to you): wherever you go, disciple the culture, change their way of life to the way of life I've taught you." [Matthew 28: 16-20]

Often, we mistakenly assume that a disciple is "a follower." It is true that Jesus called disciples to follow Him, but He called them to follow so they could be discipled. Discipling is not the same as following; it is learning how to live, think, and behave like the one who is teaching.

Discipling is learning, but not in the formal sense of merely acquiring additional information. Discipling is a process of personal change that results in the disciple being like his master. Without radical, personal, inside-out change, you cannot become the person you were created to be, nor do all you've been called to do.

Jesus says, "It is the goal of a disciple to be like his teacher." [Matthew 10:25]

Successful discipling requires good leadership. Leaders in this ministry must get you focused upon the power of the Cross and the work of Holy Spirit. To do so, they must be experiencing that power and ministry themselves, and they know how to impart that spiritual experience into you.

So, while these materials and the ministry presented is strategically designed, thoroughly Scriptural, and tested in the laboratory of real life ministry with more than 250,000 people, something more than the materials and presentation is required for this ministry to be successful. Surrender.

FreedomMinistry is about you being changed!

When discipling ministry becomes more about its leaders or methods than the Truth and Power of Christ's redemptive work and its application by Holy Spirit, the spiritual authority of salvation ministry weakens.

Discipling is a process that applies everything the Cross of Jesus provides to every believer's life and living. Certainly, God does this through leaders, but these leaders must impart spiritual experiences of Christ's work.

Discipling engages you in altering outward behavior by transforming inward conditions. Discipling is more than propagandizing saved people or teaching them to function effectively within religious structures. Discipling is nothing less than personal transformation accomplished through spiritual power and authority.

Salvation Ministry

FreedomMinistry blends several aspects of salvation ministry, incorporates insights from excellent authors, leaders, and models tested by ministry to millions, as well as successful discipling ministry from international leaders.

In other words, Dr Don has brought the best of history and ministry most powerfully impacting this generation together in FreedomMinistry!

All the elements of a life-changing experience have been combined. When the materials are used in one of FreedomMinistry's own seminars, Dr Don Lynch, or leaders personally trained by him, teach and supervise the ministry.

When FMI materials are used by others to conduct seminars, it is best if those leaders have experienced the seminars with us first and been trained by FreedomMinistry.

FreedomMinistry's Level 1 Seminar is about the Power of the Cross. Your will must be strengthened to make a "surrender decision." Get ready for personal transformation!

Personal Transformation

During this series you have the opportunity to read additional books, listen to recorded teachings, and devote yourself to personal prayer and fasting. These assignments are part of your preparation for cleansing and transformation. I urge your commitment to these assignments.

The change coming to your life will not come through the prayer and fasting of others, their revelation and commitment. You must be fully engaged in the process.

FreedomMinistry changes you. Change comes by the exercise of will. You must make decisions. So, choose to get as much as you can!

Understanding FreedomMinistry

Do not assume that you must understand everything God is doing in your life in order to receive it. Level 1 is not designed to explain everything God is doing, but to prepare you to surrender to what He is doing!

Certainly, you will understand FreedomMinistry as we teach, pray for you, fast with you, and release spiritual power and authority. However, you will not completely understand what God is doing, and you should not limit God to your own understanding if you want to get really free.

Your understanding will grow. Your faith will expand. You will be set up for surrender decisions. At each step, you must decide to surrender to the Cross.

Attend Every Session

It is very important that you attend all the sessions. The order of the sessions and the ministry that is done in each of them is sequential. Each session builds upon the other and strengthens your will to surrender.

The leadership team has walked through these experiences

themselves and with other people. While FreedomMinistry is not a program, it does build each session upon the previous one.

You will walk into a room prepared by worship and prayer. Immediately enter each session with your heart ready to worship and engage your spirit in what is happening. Get into a receiving mode so you are ready to hear His voice and receive what He is releasing.

At the end of each session, the leader will lead you in prayer. Speak with a strong, decisive voice. Make a decision. Really mean what you are praying. Believe that God has brought you to this place in life for transformation.

Strengthen Your Will

The ultimate strength of will is the strength of will to surrender. Often, you may assume that the strength of will you require to live true to your destiny is the strength of will to determine to do the right thing. You may envision gritting your teeth, clenching your fists, and buckling down 'to do the right thing.' This is not the strength of will to surrender, but the strength of will to survive.

You must be strong to survive, but you must become weak to be healed. To receive from Jesus, you must believe; and deepest faith is the surrender of the whole person, a complete reliance upon Someone outside of and greater than yourself. This seminar will strengthen your will as means to strengthening your faith.

You will never be the same again! You will become more convinced that Jesus finished atonement salvation, a salvation that provides everything you need to please God and fulfill His purpose for your life.

You must strengthen your will so you will be strong enough to let go, totally surrender your life to the power of the Cross.

Ministry Time

When the leadership team is laying hands on the participants, please do not be distracted. Do not lay hands on anyone yourself, and do not allow anyone to lay hands upon you except those designated as part of the leadership team.

Laying hands on someone is explained in the Bible, something Jesus did and taught all His disciples to do, that has continued to happen in the Church since Jesus founded His Church.

Laying on hands makes a claim on you for the kingdom of God, a gesture of spiritual authority. It does not claim you for the person ministering to you or an organization; it claims you for the kingdom of Jesus Christ. Laying on hands releases spiritual power as Holy Spirit works through people who have received and can release what they have received.

The leadership team has been trained to speak and minister with power during the ministry time. They will be gentle, but they often experience God's power and authority intensely and respond with passion and intensity as they minister. Just receive what Holy Spirit is doing in your life. They will anoint you with fragrant oil like that described in Scripture and used in Bible times. It is not magical. Anointing oil is a prophetic symbol of Holy Spirit.

At times water, cloth, clapping, or other physical things and actions will be used to help you experience physically what God is doing spiritually. Each action will be explained and every one of them is Biblical in its symbolism.

Know this: tens of thousands of people have received ministry in these ways. Even if this form of ministry is new to you or not part of your religious background, you can rest in the assurance that Dr Don has included it to illustrate how Jesus and His Church did ministry and to do ministry the way Jesus did it and taught His Church to do it.

A Personal Word from Dr Don Lynch

"We have been doing this ministry now for more than a decade and have enjoyed the awesome privilege of seeing and hearing every kind of personal issue dealt with in the power of the Cross. I have witnessed spiritual fruit in the lives of tens of thousands of men, women, and children, ***lives changed forever***!

"So, I tell you that I know whatever you have done yourself, whatever others have done to you, or whatever hell has done in your life, the power of the Cross of Jesus is greater! You will be set free, cleansed, and changed when you surrender these issues to Jesus Christ!

"The question is not whether Jesus defeated your enemies on the Cross, or whether He can heal your heart, or whether He can forgive and cleanse your sins. The question is whether or not you will decide to trust Him and *nothing else.*

"This ministry is not a magic wand. The depth of redemptive work done in you will depend upon your level of trust, your surrender to His power and authority in your life. We will be here to guide you, help you, and to release God's power and authority into your surrender, but you must make your own surrender decisions in order to appropriate the power of the Cross.

"FreedomMinistry is designed to bring freedom and maturity to your life, to deal with root issues, and teach you both how to receive freedom and how to walk in what you have received. You will never be the same!"

"Welcome to FreedomMinistry."

1
The Power of the Cross

There is power in the Cross! There is power in the Cross to redeem, to rescue, and to restore your life. There is spiritual power in the Cross, the power of heaven, the power of covenant, the power of mercy, the power of grace. Paul says the message of the Cross is the very power of God!

> *For the message of the cross is, for us who are being saved, the power of God. [1 Corinthians 1:18]*

This power is for everyone, for everything, for All. What Jesus Christ did at the Cross finished something God began before creation. The power of the Cross is the power of our covenant with God, the agreement by which He administers forgiveness, redemption, and restoration. The power of the Cross is the power to be everything you were created to be and do everything you have been called to do.

Substitution

Substitution was set in place at the very beginning of history, before Creation, at the time God decided to create all that isn't God. The Bible says Jesus is 'the Lamb offered as a sacrifice' before the world was created. Father had made a provision for substitution before Jesus created the universe and man within it.

Before Jesus created anything, in fact, He committed to die on the Cross to redeem what He was creating. (See 1 Peter 1:18-20.)

When Jesus accepted responsibility to create, He accepted responsibility to redeem. When Jesus accepted responsibility to redeem, He accepted responsibility to restore everything He created, restore it to what Father wanted it to be in the first place.

There is power in the Cross to redeem and restore everything!

"The message of the Cross comes across silly to anyone who is being lost, but we who are being rescued and delivered recognize this message of the Cross as the very power of God." [1 Corinthians 1:18]

The power of the Cross is the power of God. Paul says God has power to save anything or anyone that comes through the Cross of Jesus. The Cross releases what is necessary for salvation, and God Himself administers this power to us when we believe the Message and surrender to receive the power of the Cross.

You are Jesus' creation. You are here, now, because Father wants you. Jesus created you because you were in the Father's mind as part of Creation. Jesus accepted responsibility to get the Father what He wants. He wants you; that's why you exist! (See Revelation 5:9)

There was a time when no one knew you were there. Your momma didn't know. Your daddy didn't know.

Most certainly no one asked you if you wanted to be born! It is none of your business.

Jesus created you because Father wants you.

At that moment, when only God knew you were there, Father said, "I want that one!"

When hell became aware of you, knowing that you are Father's desire, hell said, "Whatever God wants I will do everything I can to steal, kill, and destroy."

From that moment, hell has been working to corrupt and ruin what Father wanted in your life.

But Father had a plan before Jesus created anything, a plan to redeem and restore what hell, sin, and trauma had destroyed. Father knows what He wants, and in Christ He provides a means of getting what He wants.

Because of the power of the Cross, the victory of the Resurrection, the authority of the Ascension, and the faithfulness of the Intercession of Jesus Christ, everything in the universe will finally end up exactly where it belongs. here is power in the Cross to destroy the work of hell, to forgive sins, cleanse from sin, break sin's power, set you free, and restore your destiny. (See Romans 6:5-7.)

You can be everything Jesus created you to be and do everything God has called you to do.

Spiritual Power of the Cross

God releases spiritual power in the Cross. He forgives sins—a full pardon. He breaks the power of sin—full cleansing. He defeats the claims of hell—a full freedom. He restores your destiny—a full redemption.

In fact, every sin, curse, and charge against you is defeated in the Cross. Every hold of hell is overcome by the claim Jesus made upon your life at the Cross. Because of the Cross, Jesus has the right to your life.

You do not belong to yourself, for you have been

bought with a price." [1 Corinthians 6:19-20]

However, the power of the Cross is spiritual power and only comes to you when you make a "surrender decision" to abandon yourself to its power. As long as you trust any other source or rely upon any other power, you remain in bondage in that area of your life because no other source has power to set you free. Whenever you fully trust any area of your life to the Cross, you release spiritual power greater than what hell has done to you, what you have done yourself, and what others have done to you.

Only Jesus. Only His Cross. Only His resurrection. Only His authority and kingdom. Only His intercession for you. The Cross of Jesus Christ is your only hope and help!

Your Only Source

You release the power of the Cross into your life when you surrender to it as the only source. You must strengthen your will to make surrender that deep. The highest strength of will is not the strength of will to control things yourself, but the surrendering of will to surrender them all to God.

Jesus gave one of His most definite discourses on salvation to Nicodemus, recorded in John 3. Jesus tied salvation to the Cross, describing His death with the words, "being lifted up." Jesus describes how the Cross became the point of focus for rescue and freedom.

> *Moses lifted a bronze snake up upon a pole so anyone who bitten by a poisonous snake would be healed of its deadly bite.*
>
> *"I will be lifted up just as Moses lifted up the bronze snake on a pole in the wilderness so that everyone who looks up and believes in Me will have eternal life. For God loved the world so much that He gave His only Son. To accomplish this: everyone who believes upon him will*

not perish, but have eternal life." [John 3:13-16]

Jesus says you must surrender to the power of the Cross as your only source. He refers to a story Moses told. (See Numbers 21:8-9)

While God's people are living in a desert, camping in various places, they are attacked by desert snakes. The snakes are everywhere, terrorizing God's people indiscriminately. Men, women, and children are being bitten, and everyone who is bitten dies.

Every bite is fatal. Nothing helps them the victims. No doctors. No religious ceremonies. No medicines. No sacrifices. If the snakes bit them, they would die.

Moses prays, and God tells him to make a snake of bronze and elevate it on a pole so people can see it above the tops of the tents. Moses "lifts up" this bronze snake so any person who suffers a fatal snakebite can look at the elevated bronze snake: "look and live."

God said, "Everyone who looks at the snake will be healed. Lift the snake up high so people can look at it."

Thousands of years later, Jesus says, "Just as that snake was lifted up so that anyone who looked at it would live, so I must be lifted up so anyone who believes on Me shall live." The life Jesus gives is more than physical healing; it is indestructible, spiritual life.

Jesus makes it clear that the Cross is your only source of spiritual rescue. (When we say, "saved" we are saying "rescued, delivered, salvaged," and the whole of the salvation experience flows to us from the Cross.)

The Cross overcomes every area of destruction. Any area of defeat. Any area of death. What hell is doing within you happens in a place you have failed to surrender to the power of the Cross. The victory of the Cross alone can set you free from the works of darkness and flesh.

In another instance, Paul confronted religious leaders of his generation who insisted upon religious rules and ceremonies as marks or means of salvation. He was pretty adamant about his confrontation.

> *Those who demand that you receive the rite of circumcision have one motivation; they want to avoid being persecuted for admitting that the cross of Christ alone can save. [Galatians 6:14]*

Only the Cross has power to set you free.

If hell cannot keep you from the Cross in the first place, it will do everything it can to limit the power of the Cross in your life.

You may have substituted something or someone for the Cross or simply refused or neglected to take that issue to the Cross. You will remain under that work of hell or work of flesh until you make a surrender decision to trust only Jesus and the power of His Cross.

Anything you have failed to surrender to the power of the Cross is an open door for hell to work against your destiny and calling. (We will discuss the open doors and how to close them in Session Two, "Closing the Open Doors.")

You must decide to say: "Only the Cross of Jesus Christ can save me."

Only the Cross defeats hell and the recompense of sin. Only Jesus could go to the Cross, and only the Cross can defeat sin and hell in your life.

THE SOURCE OF SPIRITUAL POWER

If you go to the doctor, you can receive what that doctor can give you. If you perform a religious ceremony, you can receive what that religious ceremony can give you. If you go to a person, you can receive only what that person can give. If you trust yourself, you can only receive what you can give yourself.

When you go to the Cross of Jesus, you receive everything Jesus can give you!

During the time Paul spent in Corinth, many people were saved. Problems arose later because people who were being saved began to choose their leaders on the basis of who baptized them in water. So Paul provides some needed apostolic leadership. He addresses this crippling division by clarifying his assignment as an apostolic leader:

> *For Christ didn't send me to baptize, but to preach the Gospel – without human wisdom and intellectual oratory—so the cross of Christ would not be limited in its power. [1 Corinthians 1:17]*

There is no substitute for the Cross. You can limit the power of the Cross in your life. When you go to the Cross of Jesus, you receive everything Jesus can give you!

At the Cross, Jesus did it all. Everything you need to be, everything you were created to be is in the Cross. Everything you need to do, everything you were called to do, is in the Cross.

Because you have a spiritual problem, you need a spiritual solution. You need spiritual power, but not just any spiritual power. (See Romans 6:10) You need the power of God and God has released His spiritual power through the Cross. There is no other place God has released His power.

> *Having begun in the Spirit, do you think you can finish in the flesh? [Galatians 3:3]*

If there were any other way, Jesus would not have died there, Father would not have given His Son there. When you substitute for the power of the Cross, you limit its power in your life and you cut yourself off from your only hope and help.

You receive the power of the Cross by believing, making

a surrender decision to trust only the Cross to forgive, to cleanse, and to restore. There is power in the Cross!

Lifting Up the Cross in Your Life

You must "lift up" the Cross in your life. The Cross and nothing else. Jesus was lifted up for you, so come to the Cross. You must say, "Only the Cross can save me."

Father gave His only Son because He is the Only One Who could take your place. He took your place on the Cross. If you could deal with the problems of sin and the works of the flesh, the works of hell, and the open doors through which hell works against your destiny, Jesus would not have needed to die.

In FreedomMinistry, you will strengthen your will so you have the strength of will to surrender. You have been strong to survive, to deal with the issues of sin, flesh, and hell in your own strength and wisdom. You have had a level of will-power that surrendered your most important issues to your own sources and solutions, but every hold hell has against your life, every claim, is broken at the Cross, and no other power can solve spiritual problems.

Behind the issues of the body and soul are spiritual roots that produce fruit: behavior, mind-set, and motivations. These spiritual roots must be removed for you to be totally free.

The Place of Judgment

Whatever issue of sin or work of hell is against you, Jesus took that issue to the Cross, and nailed it there! He could nail it there because He had victory over that issue in His own life. He took His victory to the Cross as your substitute and established His victory there for you to have victory. He took His success to the Cross to substitute for your failure. He took His purity to the Cross to substitute for your uncleanness. He nailed it there. (See Colossians 1:15-23)

Your list of accusations was erased and your arrest warrant was cancelled because Jesus took the charges against you to the Cross and nailed them there. Jesus had the right to represent you because God planned for redemption before creation. Jesus could defeat hell because hell had no charge or claim on Him.

Jesus never had rage and murder, so He could take your sinful anger, rage, and murder to the Cross and nail it there. Jesus never had lust and perversion, so He could take yours to the Cross and nail it there. Jesus never worshipped false gods, so He could take your false religion and unbelief to the Cross and nail it there. Jesus had the right to represent you, to be your substitute, to die in your place, so you could be free!

To redeem you from sin, Jesus must be sinless. To redeem you from death, Jesus must overcome death. To redeem you from hell, Jesus must defeat hell. Jesus did it—He did it all, for every man of every time. (See Colossians 2:13-15)

Your sin was judged at the Cross. God made a decision about you, a legal decision about your guilt, about whom you belong to, and about your destiny and calling, and the judgment of the Cross made His judgment about you possible: forgiven, cleansed, redeemed, regenerated, and free!

Any legal right hell has to work within you was nailed to the Cross. It is the place where the only substitute who could redeem you was offered to God as a sacrifice.

> *Since you died with Christ, you are set free from the evil powers of this world. [Colossians 2:20]*

Hell operates in your life by legal right you surrendered by personal choices or generational inheritance. Though some of your problems are not your fault, you have the opportunity to stop these operations of hell against you by taking them to the Cross. So, every day you fail to take them to the Cross, the legal right of hell to operate through them continues to stand.

The Jews hanged a person's body on a stake after they had been stoned to death to show the person was cursed by their guilt. This was the worst punishment Jewish justice could hand out.

Christ has delivered us from the recompense curse demanded by the law. When He was hung on a cross, He took upon Himself the recompense curse due us for our sins. As it is written in Scripture: "Every person who is hung upon a stake is cursed." Galatians 3:13

The Romans only crucified those who led rebellion against Roman sovereignty or runaway slaves. Jesus was nailed to the Cross because this was the worst of Roman punishment. Jesus was crucified as a rebel.

So Jesus took the worst of Jewish and Roman punishments, cursed as a Jewish rebel and crucified as a Roman rebel. In this way, He took innocence and purity, sinlessness and holiness, beauty and glory, to the Cross to gain the right and authority to pardon your rebellion against Heaven and grant you full restoration from sin, curse, rejection, shame, pride, and the work of hell against your destiny! He dealt with the curse of your sinfulness and the rebellion of your iniquity.

He has the right or authority to create you because He has the right or authority to redeem you. He knew it would require death and resurrection to make you everything He created you to be so you can do all God has called you to do.

> *You know God paid a ransom to save you from the empty lifestyle you inherited from your ancestors; the ransom He paid was not perishable gold or silver. It was the priceless blood of Christ, the Lamb of God who had no sin or defect. God chose Him to be your ransom long before the world began. [1 Peter 1:18-19]*

To redeem from sin, Jesus must remain victorious over sin, and die a sinless man. To redeem from death, Jesus must overcome death. To redeem from hell, Jesus must defeat hell. (See Hebrews 9:14) In this way, He gained the right or authority to remove sin by the cleansing power of His blood. He gained the right or authority to remove the claim of hell on your life by defeating the ultimate enemy, the last claim of hell. Death.

Christ suffered for our sins once for all time. He never sinned, but He died for sinners to bring you safely home to God. He suffered physical death, but He was raised to life in the Spirit. [1 Peter 3:18]

In other words, if He defeated the ultimate enemy, death, you can be assured that every other enemy is certainly under His feet or authority. In the Cross and Resurrection, Jesus defeated every work of hell.

Jesus did everything, once and for all, that needed to be done to redeem every man and everything. In the Cross, redemption is finished forever.

When you surrender any area of your life to the power of the Cross, His victory and authority defeats every work of hell in that area of your life.

Declaring the Power of the Cross

In this session, you are going to declare that the power of the Cross defeats every right or authority for hell to operate in your life. You will repent for substituting human wisdom and strength for the power of the Cross. You will renounce the substitutes and begin surrendering your spiritual issues to the power of the Cross.

You must exercise your will, make a surrender decision, and declare your decision. You must strengthen your will to be strong enough to surrender. This is your faith decision, your surrender decision, to make the Cross your only source of redemption and freedom.

To the extent you are strong enough to surrender yourself and your issues to the power of the Cross, to that extent you have released the power of the Cross to redeem, restore, and release your true destiny.

You must surrender all. You are dealing with spiritual issues; and until you have surrendered those issues in the spirit, you are dealing with spiritual issues by the strength and wisdom of flesh. You are, in fact, substituting something else for the power of the Cross in your life.

> *Since you died with Christ, you are set free from the evil powers of this world. [Colossians 2:20]*

When Jesus defeated hell, He defeated its right to operate in your life, but you must decide to give Him authority in every area of life. You only gain authority over the work of hell in Jesus, in the Cross, not in yourself.

Stop limiting the Power of the Cross!

If hell cannot keep you from the Cross in the first place, hell will do everything it can to limit the power of the Cross in your life. If hell cannot keep you from being born again, hell will do whatever it can to keep spiritual power from transforming your life and living.

By making the Cross a symbol, a fetish, a religious relic, hell will change its meaning and keep you from the spiritual crucifixion you need.

> *So that the Cross may not be emptied of, or limited in, its power. [1 Corinthians 1:17]*

Paul says it is possible to limit the power of the Cross, to frustrate its power. If the Cross is not real, not the source and resource of your redemption, not the only hope and help of your life, the Scripture "I am crucified with Christ" becomes a mere motto instead of a lifestyle. There is a constant, consistent effort upon the part of hell to limit and frustrate the power of the Cross in my life.

Paul also mentions people whose religious lifestyle and teaching actually makes them enemies of the Cross; people who believe they are serving God by works are trying to maintain control of their redemption. This is not something "close to Christianity" or something that "at least heads the right direction." It is a substitute for the power of the Cross. It is another Gospel altogether foreign to the Bible according to Paul.

A religious substitution takes on a spiritual life of its own. It is a spiritual condition that we call "a spirit of religion." It is an enemy of the Cross because it substitutes the strength and wisdom of man for the power and authority of the Cross. If something I can do redeems me, Jesus would not have died, faced down hell, and conquered my enemies. The deception of the religious spirit is that it sounds like, smells like, looks like, and feels like the work of God while it is nothing more than a substitute for the Cross.

> *Those who want you to receive the rite of circumcision want to look good to others. They don't want to be persecuted for teaching that the Cross of Christ alone can deliver. [Galatians 6:12]*

The Scripture says that substitutes for the Cross like human ideas and activities alienate me from the Cross. They separate me from the only source that can set me free, cleanse my soul and defeat my enemies. While I trust my allegiance to any work of man, I am limiting, frustrating, and substituting the work of God, the power of the Cross that is the power of God.

I remain enslaved, not free. I remain polluted, not cleansed. I remain the same, not changed. This religious activity does nothing to pay the price of my pardon, provide spiritual cleansing, or defeat my spiritual enemies.

So, I must repent and renounce my substitutes and embrace the Cross as my only source, help, and hope. My redemption and restoration do not depend upon my efforts; they depend upon what Jesus did at the Cross.

During these sessions you will strengthen your will, surrender your rights, and make the Cross your only source and resource for redeeming, restoring, and releasing your destiny.

Strengthen Your Will to Surrender

When you surrender, you will never be the same again! You will be more convinced that Jesus finished atonement salvation and that what He did provides everything you need to please God and fulfill His purpose for your life!

This surrender is the very essence of faith, for faith is a constant surrender, receiving from Jesus Christ what I can never earn or acquire on my own or from any other source or resource. Faith requires the greatest risk.

> *God in His wisdom understood that the world could never know Him by means of human wisdom; He decided to use foolish preaching (of the Cross) to save everyone who believes. It is foolish to Jews who require signs from heaven. It is foolish to non-Jews who value human wisdom. We proclaim Christ crucified - to those who are called by God, Christ is the power and wisdom of God. [1 Corinthians 1:21]*

Nothing you can do or have done saves you or any part of your life from sin, curse, and the work of hell. On the other hand, nothing you can do or have done destroys your destiny or puts you so far away that God forgets you or cannot bring you back. The Cross is enough to do what you cannot; and, the Cross has enough power to fully redeem and restore your destiny!

Many Christians live as if Christ saves them but has little or nothing to do with their lives and living after they are born again.

You need the power of the Cross to begin new life, and you need the power of the Cross continually to live the new life you have received. You must strengthen your will so you will be strong enough to let go, totally surrender your life to the power of the Cross.

The Bible never treats the Cross as a symbol. Although the Cross is part of real history, it is more than history. There is power in the Cross!

Boasting in the power of the Cross is boasting of its power to forgive, cleanse, restore, and release everything created to its fulfillment and purpose. Boasting in the Cross is declaring that it is the only source of spiritual power and authority for every spiritual need of my life.

> *As for me, may I never boast of anything except the Cross of our Lord Jesus Christ. In His Cross I am crucified to the world and its claim upon me. [Galatians 6 :14]*

When I boast of my religious activities or myself, I have a fabricated source of my redemption. And, when I fabricate this source, I am deceived; no substitute can ever defeat my enemies or cleanse my soul! Boasting is a way of declaring what I believe and trust.

When Paul was talking about boasting in the Cross, he was discussing the hold of religion or human wisdom and strength, trusting in what I have done or not done as a source of being right with God. He says, What I have done or not done means nothing; what is vital is a new creation, a new nature created in me by Jesus Christ.

Boasting is saying something, and we must understand that

saying something is necessary to spiritual change. We must speak our decision, declare, confess, repent, boast, or praise. We gotta say sumthin'!

Boasting declares how it is: because we believe the reality of what Jesus has done in the spirit and trust that spiritual power and authority we declare it.

For if you confess out loud that Jesus is Lord and believe, trust, and surrender in your heart to the fact that God raised Him from among the dead, you will be saved, set free, and delivered. For it is by believing in your heart that you are made right with God, and it is by confessing with your mouth that you are saved, set free, and delivered. As the Scriptures tell us, "Anyone who believes in him will not be disappointed. [Romans 10:9-11]

Jesus defeated your enemies! Your enemy operates within you because he has gained some legal right to do so. Your enemy uses that legal position to accuse you, operate within you, and defeat and deceive you until you cancel those rights by an authority greater than you and your enemy. Within yourself, you don't have the power and authority to defeat hell. Hell has a legal right to control aspects of your soul until that right is cancelled.

By defeating your spiritual enemies, Jesus gained the right to remove their control from any and every area of your life. He had the right to be a substitute for you and died for you. He has gained the right or authority over every work of hell.

Now, you must say something. Make a decision and say something. You must surrender your rights because you are not strong enough to defeat your enemies. You must decide to make Jesus Lord, give Him control, surrender your rights to yourself to Him because His authority is greater than the authority of hell.

He canceled the proof of the charges against us and took the charges away, nailing it to the Cross. In this way, He stripped the spiritual rulers and authorities of their claims, shaming them publicly by His victory over them in the Cross. [See Colossians 2:14-15.]

He made a public display of the defeat of your enemies—in the Cross—where He triumphed over them, where He disarmed hell's rulers and governors, removing their claims to us, claims that allowed them to control our bondage or imprisonment, or call for us to pay our debts to them.

This Scripture pictures a public parade of a returning, victorious army led by the General who has won the victory. In this case, the whole army is One Man who is leader, victor, and champion. Yes, a parade of defeated enemies led by One Man is moving along in a public display of victory.

The cheers should be loud! A boasting. A celebration. A public display of the obvious. The enemies are seen humiliated, defeated, weak, powerless, and under the control of the Champion. This is boasting in the Cross.

Jesus Christ did something at the Cross that changed forever how things are in the spirit, and that finished work of redemption is your redemption. You are free from the control and bondage of hell because of Jesus Christ. Your only boast and celebration is the power of the Cross.

RECEIVING PRAYER MINISTRY

Now, we will repeat prayers of repentance, renunciation, and declaration. And, as you exercise your will in speaking, the power of the Cross will be released within you. In repentance, you change to be changed.

You will come forward to receive prayer ministry from trained leaders. Your own words witness to your decision, and the prayer ministry seals those words and allows us to join in agreement with spiritual power and authority, laying hands on you to release the kingdom of God.

Jesus did it. Jesus taught His disciples to do it, and He said the Church would continue to do it until He returns.

So, receive this ministry of anointing prayer as Holy Spirit applies the power of the Cross to your life. You will experience the reality of what God is doing. You will be changed. You are choosing the power of the Cross, the Blood of Jesus, and the work of Holy Spirit.

It is powerful! Tens of thousands of others have received this breakthrough prayer ministry.

So, speak with a strong voice without shouting or screaming, speak with conviction and faith, declare these prayers as we repent, renounce, rebuke, and receive.

What is spiritual is more real than what is physical. You are a spiritual being. Your soul controls your life, your body and brain, your speech, and your behavior. When hell operates against you, it does so spiritually. Hell works against your life through your soul.

In the next section, you are going to uncover how hell opens doors through which to operate in your soul. You will repent and renounce the legal right hell has gained, the right to operate within your soul, and you will begin closing open doors to the work of hell in your life. We will close the doors that allow the work of hell in our lives!

But now, we are going to repent, renounce, and break off our substitutes for the power of the Cross.

It is powerful! Tens of thousands of others have received this breakthrough prayer ministry. So, speak with a strong voice without shouting or screaming, speak with conviction and faith, declare these prayers as we repent, renounce, rebuke, and receive.

THE POWER OF THE CROSS

2

Closing Open Doors

How does hell gain the legal right to operate within you or within your life? How does someone spiritual alive by new birth still experience the influence of hell from inside? What are "open doors" and how do they provide opportunity for the work of hell? And, most importantly, how do you close those doors and shut hell out of our life?

An "open door" means you have given or allowed hell the right or authority to operate in your life. As long as you tolerate that right, you are surrendering to its authority. The door was opened, and you have allowed it to remain open. The enemy has taken advantage of this opportunity to continue to establish his influence and control.

Some doors were opened by trauma, abuse, and violation when you were vulnerable; they were opened by what was done to you, not through your sins, and the occasion of these doors opening were not even your fault. Yet, as long as you tolerated that work, even though it wasn't your fault initially, you were the one keeping the door open.

Sin opened doors for hell to operate in you. Your sins gave

hell legal right because you made decisions, exercised your will, and opened the doors on purpose. You yielded ground to hell, and hell kept pushing the boundaries to gain more ground. Your sins grew and established dominions in your soul. You became a victim of hell's controlling darkness.

This is true of any person who yields to temptation and iniquity. Spiritual doors are opened. Opportunities are created for hell to establish the right to operate in them.

For you to be free, you must exercise your will. Your decision must be to take these spiritual issues to the Cross. You do not have the spiritual power or authority to break the bondage. That is, even when you make the decision to cancel any right hell has to operate within you, you must appropriate the power of the Cross to remove hell's right and close that open door.

Spiritual Doors

If we begin at the beginning, the very first baby ever born, we see a vivid picture of open doors. Adam and Eve, the first man and woman called their firstborn son, "Cain."

Cain was a farmer. His brother, Abel, was a shepherd. When the two brothers brought an offering, God received Abel's and refused Cain's. This made Cain angry.

God spoke to Cain and gave him insight about open doors, of how hell seeks to work within man, waiting for man to open a door that so hell gains the right to work inside.

> *The Lord asked him, "Why are you so angry? Why do you look so rejected? You will be accepted if you do right; but if you insist upon your own way, beware that sin crouches at the door, waiting to attack and destroy you, and you must rule over it." [Genesis 4:6-7]*

This is the very first use of the word "sin" in Scripture. God speaks the word and reveals how things work in the spirit. "Sin crouches at the door." The picture: a waiting enemy crouched and ready to jump in when a door opens, a panther prepared to pounce. One ancient translation reads, "A demon is waiting to get in."

God tells Cain that his obedience to God will put him in a position of dominion over this effort of hell to influence and control him because his offering will be accepted when it sheds blood, but Cain refused to worship as God had designed worship to be done. Cain wanted God to change worship to fit Cain's design; so, he brought God what he wanted God to have instead of bringing God what God wanted. Rebellion and religion were operating in the first son ever born!

Points of Entry

God warns that disobedience gives hell an opening to work within us. Hell enters to gain influence within us just as satan had sought and gained an opening within Eve and Adam in the Garden. Sin opens doors to the work of hell in our lives.

Our sinful life opens many doors. Hell builds "strongholds," or places of control and influence inside us through them, and operates within us when we surrender to its demanding desires, or "lusts." These strongholds shape our dispositions, personalities, and relationships, influencing our behavior.

These points of entry must be closed. The process of reclaiming our entire lives begins when we are born anew and spiritual life begins. Our spirit becomes the place of strength, power, and authority, the entry point for Holy Spirit to control and influence our lives. The process of reclaiming, rescuing, and restoring our true selves is called "redemption." Part of redemption brings destruction to hell's strongholds, removes legal rights, and closes open doors.

We are going to begin closing all the open doors to the work of hell within us!

No Claim on Me

Jesus spent the night before His death with His disciples. After dinner, they walked toward the garden together. Here, during that last night, Jesus would pray to Father and surrender Himself to the Cross.

As they are walking along, Jesus shared what was about to happen.

> *I will not be talking with you like this anymore, for the prince of this world is coming. But don't worry, he has nothing in Me. [John 14:30]*

The devil is the prince of this world, and he was arriving to finish a sinister plot to destroy Jesus.

Note what Jesus says: "he has nothing in Me." Jesus had no open doors to the work of hell in His life! Without sin, never falling victim to the work of hell, never tolerating hell's attempts through temptation and trial to gain entrance into His life, Jesus walked with Father in perfect fellowship, without sin. So, hell could gain no right to operate within Jesus.

Now, hell did work very hard against Jesus from the outside through temptation and attempts to destroy, discredit, and distress Him. A whole list of hellish strategies could be written to recount the effort of hell working from the outside. But hell never had even one open door within Jesus.

Basically, Jesus is saying, "Don't worry satan has no claim in Me."

Jesus carried a sinless life to the Cross. He lived holy, without sin, and has no innate sinfulness. Against every strategy of hell to destroy Him, He remains untarnished. Jesus had no open doors. He was tempted, abused, opposed, rejected, belittled, betrayed, tortured, and killed, but nothing hell threw at Him stuck.

He is the Champion because He was victor over all enemies—your enemies. Having faced everything you face and never opening doors through sin, unforgiveness, lust, anger, gossip, greed, or works of flesh, He gives you victory over those same enemies. As your substitute, He took His victory to the Cross. At the Cross, Jesus gained the right and authority to close all the doors open to the work of hell in your life.

No door can remain open to hell once you surrender it to the Cross of Jesus Christ.

HE DESTROYS THE WORKS OF HELL

As you take these places of spiritual defeat to the Cross, cancelling the right of hell to operate in any area of your life, the doors are closed. Jesus can close any door through which hell operates in your life.

> *By God's grace Jesus tasted death for everything. It was proper that God who made everything and for whom everything was made would make Jesus complete through suffering, the ultimate source and pioneer bringing many children into Glory. [Hebrews 2:9]*

Literally, this Scripture tells us that Christ's victory cancels hell's right and authority to any place, person, or condition. Everything. Jesus redeemed everything He created when He died on the Cross, and He gained the authority and power to close every open door in your life!

> *But the Son of God was revealed to destroy the works of the devil. [1 John 3:8]*

There is something destructive about redemption. Something is demolished by the power of the Cross. Jesus broke down the gates of hell and destroyed the works of hell. He has the authority and power to do this in your life.

Jesus is not talking about spring cleaning! He will destroy what the devil has done in you through these open doors, remove the right of hell to operate within you, and close the doors. You can have the open doors closed forever!

Recompense

Some of the open doors were established as a curse. A "curse" is a recompense operating in your life that gives hell a legal right to operate against your destiny. Curses arrive through the generations upon the land, people, and nations through various sins like cursing Israel as a nation, idolatrous worship, or for failure to give God what belongs to Him.

Curse means recompense. Something is due that needs to be paid. Spiritual accounting shows something due to God. Curses for iniquity give satan legal right in the spirit to operate and release destruction.

Many recompenses are mentioned in the Bible. Sin itself causes a curse because it requires and demands a reward. The wages of sin is death. Death is one such curse, a recompense that came upon humanity in the garden of Eden.

Jesus redeems us from curse! His death satisfies the recompense or demanded reward. Curses are not automatically broken just because Jesus died however, anymore than sins are forgiven because He provided pardon. The Cross must be applied to curse by a surrender decision.

We are not talking about foul language per se when we speak of curse or cursing, even though we refer to foul language as "curse words." We are not talking about witchcraft hexes sometimes referred to as curses. (The definition of curse in witchcraft does not fit the definition of curse in the Scriptures. Witchcraft seeks to use spiritual power to get something; the use of hex is an effort to inflict destruction through the power of hell.)

Curse in the Bible simply means something is owed. We could not pay what was owed except through our own deaths, but for us to die without Christ's resurrection meant that we had no hope. Our death would merely pay what we owed, make things even, but would not afford us eternal life. Our death couldn't redeem us; it would merely destroy us. We would be dead without redemption from death. Our debt would be paid, but our lives forever forfeited.

In order for redemption to release eternal life, someone who could not only die but conquer death as well, must pay the death debt owed! Jesus Christ alone had the capacity to do that, and He did it at the Cross!

> *Christ has redeemed us from the curse of the law. There He Himself became a curse for us: For it is written, 'Everyone hung upon a tree is cursed.' [Galatians 3:13]*

Jesus took upon Himself the curse, put it upon His back, and carried it to His Cross. Jesus has the power and authority to release you from every recompense, break every curse, and remove any legal right of hell to bring destruction to your life.

Breaking the curse closes the open door. We need to break these legal rights in the power of the Cross.

Spiritual Agreements

Agreements made in the spirit are real and binding. They establish places for demonic activity. These agreements continue to operate as long as we continue to tolerate them, surrender to them, and live with them. Your agreement with the enemy is a surrender of rights. Sin opens the doors. Wounds open the doors. Traumas open the doors. Do not give the devil any opportunity. Open doors give hell legal rights to work within you.

Jesus says, "The thief comes only to steal, kill, and destroy." So when you open the door, you are welcoming hell into sacred places to steal, kill, and destroy.

Jesus created you to possess the very things hell wants to steal. Jesus created you to live as the very person hell wants to kill. Jesus created you to minister and lead with the very attributes hell wants to destroy.

You leave the doors open because you fail to recognize them as points of entry. You are a victim of hell's deception.

Most of the doors were opened when you were young, ignorant, vulnerable, and you surrendered rights to hell without understanding the consequences.

You received the lie. You believed the lie. You lived the lie.

Even now, you may be welcoming some of hell's worst deceptions and strategies to defeat you into your life! Stop agreeing with your enemies! Stop putting out a welcome mat for hell to operate in your life!

STOP AGREEING WITH YOUR ENEMY

You are opening the doors willingly, surrendering, and tolerating the work of your adversary. You are making room for demons. You are puffing up your pillow so your favorite demon will be comfortable sleeping in your bed.

That's why you continue to act up and experience destructive cycles of behavior. That's why you remain controlled by anger, lust, fear, or greed. That's why the abuse of your childhood still defines how you respond in relationships today. That's why strongholds of unbelief, religion, pornography, and witchcraft still operate in your soul.

Stop agreeing with your enemy. Stop tolerating his lies, deceptions, and works of darkness!

You need to close those doors by removing the right of hell to operate within you. You need to cancel the legal agreements, the surrenders, and the tolerations of your enemy.

In this session, you will begin closing these doors. You will never be the same again!

When Paul says not to give the devil an opportunity, the word he uses means both time and place. That is, an opportunity can be a place where the devil has a right to work or a time surrendered to his influence. The word refers to making room for the devil by 'giving him the time of day' or allowing him space to operate.

> *Do not give the devil a place of opportunity. [Ephesians 4:27]*

Stop behaviors that open the door to the work of hell. Stop entertainment, relationship, habits, sins, and conversation that give satan a place to sit down and stay awhile. You do not need "to give the devil a chance" as if the rules of the game require "fair play" opportunities for the work of hell. You don't owe the devil anything, but you have tolerated and surrendered places in your life to him that he doesn't want to give up. You don't deserve to suffer because of what you've done.

You don't have to give the enemy "the time of day." Don't listen. Don't allow demonic distraction. Don't try to become an expert in darkness with the misplaced notion that you will be able to defeat darkness with your deep insights. This is a trap of pride.

Change your lifestyle and behavior so that nothing in your life opens a door for the work of hell.

You ask, "How could I be leaving a door open? How could I be putting a welcome mat at the door of my life? I don't want hell in my house, in my finances, marriage, or soul."

Don't Tolerate Evil

You do not have to tolerate the work of hell in your life. In fact, Jesus has given you complete, overcoming victory, and He is not pleased when you ignore what He has provided.

Once you have become part of the kingdom of God, you must reject, cleanse, and remove any claims of the kingdom of darkness. There is no room in God's people for the work of hell!

> *Do not yield any body part as a tool or weapon for wickedness. Instead, yield yourselves completely to God since you are living a raised-from-the-dead life. Yield your whole body as a tool or weapon to God for what is right. Don't you realize whatever you surrender to becomes your master? You can choose to obey sin (that produces death), or you can choose to obey God and do right. [Romans 6:13, 16]*

When John saw Jesus walking among the churches in the Revelation, he heard Jesus say against one of the churches, "You tolerate that falsely prophetic woman, Jezebel."

The leaders and people of that church ignored the work of deception and witchcraft this false prophet did among them, did not exercise the authority and power the Cross and Holy Spirit provides to cleanse her influence and power from the church. Many were hurt, wounded, and deceived by her false leadership.

The principle is that Jesus does not tolerate the work of hell, and He is not interested in you doing so either. He will not ignore what you are willing to ignore. He died to destroy the works of the devil. He died to cleanse His people from the influences of deception. He is shining light on the works of darkness so they can be removed from His church.

You can't afford to "tune out" the reality of spiritual oppression, demonic operations, and the work of hell in your life. If you tolerate hell's operations, you are already deceived. You have received the lie, believed the lie, and are living the lie that somehow it won't matter or that "it is not that bad a problem."

These works of hell are invaders, intruders, and interlopers on God's property. Begin closing the doors to the work of hell in your life! Jesus will never stop until every claim of hell is revealed and destroyed in your life!

Redeem It or Destroy It?

One way Christians tolerate the work of hell in their lives is by unwittingly bringing idols into their homes. They seem harmless, perhaps, when you purchase them as mementos, art, or souvenirs, but they are not harmless. They are welcome mats that create legal rights for demons to live with you!

The Bible makes it clear that behind every idol is a demon spirit, a hellish being that has legal rights to operate in the lives of people who willingly possess that idol. (See 1 Corinthians 10:18-2) Modern people often fail to see or recognize idols, or dedicated things, for what they are.

Dedicated things have a purpose or spiritual claim attached to them. Some dedicated things can be redeemed. Jewelry, art, gifts. Things given or acquired with special meaning, the purpose of giving or receiving having a spiritual significance, carry a spiritual claim upon them. When you volunteer to receive them, display them, hang them on the wall, own and possess them, you are volunteering to allow the spiritual purpose or claim attached to them entry into your life. Often, these dedicated things can be redeemed through repentance and renunciation of the claims.

Idols are different. Idols cannot be redeemed. They must be destroyed. They are works of man specifically designed and manufactured to represent a false god, a substitute for the God of the Bible. Every idol has a demon spirit behind it. Receiving, purchasing, possessing, or displaying idols is a wide open door to the work of that demon in your life.

> *Am I saying that the animals sacrificed to idols by non-Jews are valuable or make the idols what they think they are? No, but the sacrifices to idols are offered to demons, not to God. And I don't want any of you to share*

in the worship of demons. You cannot drink from the Lord's cup and the demons' cup. You cannot eat from the Lord's table and the table of demons, too! Do you want to stir the Lord's jealousy? [1 Corinthians 10:19-22]

While dedicated items may sometimes be redeemed, idols must be destroyed. Every idol. Every time. Idols are not redeemable.

You should repent for receiving and possessing the idol, renounce the claim and right you gave the demonic spirit behind it, and break and destroy the idol. You should get rid of what's left.

Items could be stored in a trunk from foreign service in wars, brought back from trips to other nations, given or passed down by relatives, or purchased at a department store as art. They may be worth a lot of money or valued as a memento or heirloom; still, they must be renounced and destroyed if they are idols to close the open door.

Some physical objects from previous relationships, marriages, and affairs may still and spiritual claims within your soul because you are not breaking the soul ties of the past. Repent and renounce those claims.

Some objects are left over from your sinful lifestyle that should be destroyed because they are spiritual links to previous addictions and sin. You need to clean house spiritually to close the open doors hell.

Cleaning house, smashing idols, and redeeming items from the spiritual claim left upon them does not mean that you are solving the problem. It means that you are breaking the claim of hell by making a surrender decision and saying words with spiritual effect.

The power of the idol or item is broken by the power of the Cross. So, you must appropriate that power through repentance.

Repentance Closes the Door

Repentance breaks the legal right. We will repent, renounce, and break the legal right of hell to operate through an open door. Pardon does not close the open door; even though you were forgiven for the sin committed, the open door must be closed. It is certain the lust operating in your life will not be removed when you continue in pornography, fornication, lewd behavior, or adultery; and, the open door isn't closed through confession and pardon of sin else the vicious cycle wouldn't continue so that confession of the same behaviors is repeated again and again.

In our next session, "The Discipline of Repentance," we will learn that repentance means, "I change to be changed." The Bible says we should produce the fruit of repentance. That means we should have a changed behavior when we have a changed heart.

Repentance closes the open door. Repentance begins life changes that remove the legal right of hell to operate. Repentance is an exercise of your will that includes renouncing the legal right of hell. When you take the issues of your life—what you've done, what's been done to you, and what hell is doing in your life right now—to the Cross, repentance releases spiritual power to break hell's hold and set you free!

No matter how long the door has been open. No matter how the door was opened in the first place. No matter how many times you have committed the sin, gone through the cycle, or surrendered to the deception. No matter how horrible the sin you've done or has been done to you.

There is power in the Cross to set you free of any and every legal right of hell to operate in your life and to close every open door!

We will speak extensively about repentance in our next section, "Exercising the Discipline of Repentance," and you will discover repentance as your new, favorite thing to do! Repentance appropriates the power of the Cross. Repentance releases grace. Repentance sets you up for transformation! Inside out.

Receiving Prayer Ministry

Now, we will repeat prayers of repentance, renunciation, and declaration. We've gotta say somethin'!

And, as you exercise your will in speaking, the power of the Cross will be released within you to close the open doors. In repentance, you change to be changed.

You will begin closing doors. Perhaps there are idols and items in your life that need to be removed and destroyed or redeemed. You will commit to life-change and house cleaning, to deal with those issues.

You will come forward to receive prayer ministry from trained leaders. Your own words witness to your decision, and the prayer ministry seals those words and allows us to join in agreement with spiritual power and authority, laying hands on you to release the kingdom of God.

Jesus did it. Jesus taught His disciples to do it, and He said the Church would continue to do it until He returns.

So, receive this ministry of anointing prayer as Holy Spirit applies the power of the Cross to your life. You will experience the reality of what God is doing. You will be changed. You are choosing the power of the Cross, the Blood of Jesus, and the work of Holy Spirit.

It is powerful! Tens of thousands of others have received this breakthrough prayer ministry.

So speak with a strong voice without shouting or screaming, speak with conviction and faith, declare these prayers as we repent, renounce, rebuke, and receive.

3

THE DISCIPLINE OF REPENTANCE

I confess to be forgiven; I repent to be changed. Repentance means, I change to be changed. The change occurs inside and produces changes in behavior outside.

Confession is powerful!

When I confess sin, Father forgives me because of the Cross. There is power in the Cross to pardon any, every, and all sins! All. However, confession is not repentance.

Many people live a life of sin-confession, expecting to continue doing the same sins; they live as victims of sin, controlled by sin—anger, lust, lying, greed, hate, fear, and others. They cycle through depression, bitterness, rejection, pride, then confession and forgiveness, only to cycle back through the sins with more confession, relief, testing, and failure.

REPENTANCE BREAKS CYCLES

Behavior is based upon habits. As much as 90% of behavior is nearly automatic, based upon attitudes, or habits and patterns of thinking. These attitudes are based upon a mindset of values and beliefs that answers to a basic personal philosophy of life.

Repentance affects behavior by changing the internals: it alters the fundamentals of mind and will, the patterns that habitually respond to life in attitude and habits of behavior.

Paul says, "Change our mind-set." Change the basis upon which you see yourself, make decisions, and form habits, attitudes, and behavior.

> *Stop shaping your life by this world [or allowing it to shape you], instead, be changed inside out, behavior-change based upon a changed mind; in this way, prove what God wants, what is good to Him, what makes Him happy, and what ultimately finishes His purpose in your destiny. [Romans 12:2]*

When your mind-set is different, you behave differently because you think differently.

When repentance opens your inner man to the power of the Cross, Holy Spirit brings spiritual control and motivation to your thinking and actions, and you begin to respond to life as a changed person. This is true freedom, freedom to experience lasting life-change and ultimate identity change.

It is time to break the cycles of sin, failure, fear, and lust! Stop the cycles of regret, shame, pride, and rejection.Although saved, you keep acting up. It is time to change to be changed!

There is more to being saved than having your sins forgiven. Salvation pardons, cleanses, and restores.

God will forgive, and you should continue to confess to be pardoned every time you sin. Jesus says, "All sin shall be forgiven." So, your sin, no matter how terrible, ugly, or how often repeated, will be forgiven when you confess.Every time.

Full pardon is available in the power of the Cross. However, God is after more. He wants to break sin's power in your life, and release full restoration of the person He created you to be.

Turn Around

The word "repentance" means a fundamental change of mind. "I changed my mind" has a more flippant connotation in American speech, implying momentary whim or shallow compulsion.

The intent of the word in Scripture is significant: repentance means a fundamental change of the way I think about something that changes the way I behave and respond.

Two Greek words combine to form this word "repentance." Together, they carry the sense of "after changing one's mind or feeling or perception." There is a sense of the continued working and application of the change of mind that begins a new point of reference, to change one's purpose or redefine one's viewpoint. Change comes because I choose to believe new revelation, and choose to change the motivations behind my behaviors. Repentance means, "I was going one way and made a complete turnaround, and now I am going in the opposite or a new direction."

New revelation challenges your thinking and demands a change of mind. A changed mind challenges your habits of thinking and acting, and demands changed behavior. Your decision to accept this new viewpoint leads to a transformation so you can live consistent with what you now believe to be true. And, spiritual power is available in your redeemed life that gives you the capacity to do and live what God has promised!

So, repentance demands a change of behavior because nothing else is consistent with my changed mind. Once Truth has come, I must repent—change my thinking—or I must deny what I now know to be true as basis for obedience.

Inside-Out

Repentance is not only a "turn around and go the other way" change. It is also an "inside-out," spiritual change. The change begins inside to alter behavior outside. Repentance is a surrender decision that begins in the soul. It assumes more than pardon will occur. It demands change of heart and mind to release grace and spiritual power on God's part.

God exposes areas of personal need, the places you need to change, and repentance releases the strategy of Holy Spirit to change you. The change comes because your repentance surrenders those places to the power of the Cross.

Until you have surrendered, you are dealing with these issues. Your surrender decision allows Holy Spirit to deal with them in the power of the Cross. When you deal with them, you release what you can do; when you surrender them to the Cross, you release what God can do.

In this way, repentance sets you up for change: I change to be changed. The power of the Cross cannot change you as long as you continue to deal with your issues. You are making your own wisdom and strength the source and resource of your life.

If you could change yourself, the Cross would not have been necessary. You need Someone who has overcome, Someone with the power and authority of victory to set you free!

> *Through Jesus, God brought everything back to Himself. He made peace between everything—in heaven and on earth through His blood shed upon the Cross. Including you who were once so far away from God, His enemies, separated by your hostile mind and evil actions. Now He has brought you back. He has done this through the death of His own body on the Cross. [Colossians 2:20-22]*

Jesus is your Champion because He took your issues to the Cross, took your place there, conquered those issues for you, and became your source and resource for personal life-change!

Repentance sets you up to receive what Jesus did for you on the Cross. Repentance releases the grace of the Cross into your life!

THE GRACE OF THE CROSS

The term "grace" is used in many ways in the Bible. While it is improper to make the term mean the same thing every time it is used, we can speak of grace in the redemptive sense, the Divine sense, as an endowment or capacity of power and strength.

Grace usually refers to something given, unearned or developed by the one receiving it. Grace is given. By grace, you are someone you could not be or can do something you could not do without grace. In the New Testament we can read "grace" as "power."

Grace means "gift or given" but when given by God, it means power to be and do something only God could empower you to be and do. Grace comes from Jesus, your Source and Resource, who gives you what you don't have on your own.

> *For the law was given through Moses. Grace and truth arrived through Jesus Christ. [John 1:17]*

Grace comes through surrender. You cannot earn it, control it, or produce it. You receive it and release it through a surrender.

Like Truth, which you cannot find on your own by research or discovery, Holy Spirit must release grace which you cannot develop or produce through your own effort. Grace and truth arrived through Jesus. Grace is received. Truth is revealed. Then, you learn to walk in, live in, and behave on the basis of spiritual grace enabling.

Grace contrasts with law. Keeping rules can be accomplished with the mind and will of man. This is religion or life lived in your own control, under the law: doing what I understand is right, even for the wrong reason, with whatever level of success my human strength and wisdom allows me.

> *Sin is no longer your master. You're not bound under it any longer, but free under grace. [Romans 6:14]*

Many, many Christians have mistaken grace for mercy. They may even have been taught that grace means God "overlooks sin" or that the Blood of Jesus merely covers over my sin so God can't see it. Yet grace is not mercy, but the enabling power of Holy Spirit to do what God expects as norms for His kingdom culture.

Mercy is fundamentally about time in the salvation sense. Without mercy, God would simply send you to hell the first time you sin, and be just in doing so. He doesn't because He is merciful.

God gives time for repentance and change. Though it appears that God is not looking at my sin, He appears to ignore it—because He doesn't kill me the moment I commit sin—He is giving me time to change, not ignoring my sin. This is not grace but mercy.

The term "grace" means given and received as a capacity to accomplish a purpose fulfill a destiny. Grace brings Truth into fullness, what God revealed He wanted is done through the grace you receive to do it.

This is what Jesus meant about the law: "I didn't come to destroy the Law or prophets but to fulfill them." (Matthew 5) So, Jesus didn't come to do away with what God wants, He came to perfectly do everything God wants by means of an inside-out, spiritual transformation.

His perfect life, nailed to the Cross, provides spiritual strength and power for you to become more like Jesus, receiving a grace flow to be and do what God wants.

Grace is power! Grace is strength! Grace enables you to do something you could never do without it. Grace enables you to be someone you could never be without it.

Repentance releases the grace of the Cross to any area you open to its power. Your surrender decision in that area of your life destroys works of flesh and works of hell and establishes the righteousness of Jesus!

Changed Behavior

Repentance is not "I'm so sorry I got caught." It is a decision to change, a transforming decision that opens that area of my life to the power of the Cross.

John arrived preaching repentance. He says, "Get ready. Change your behavior. Someone is coming soon who will take that life-change to another level, a level of transformation far beyond what my leadership and spiritual power can produce in you."

John baptized in water. His baptism was valid as a prophetic action, anticipating Jesus' ministry. It is still valid today. I am submerged into water to denote the death and burial of the old life. I am lifted up out of the water to denote the beginning of a new life.

John says, "Produce the fruit of repentance if you are baptized in water. Don't just do this as a ritualistic show." (Matthew 3)

The fruit of repentance is changed behavior. John insisted that repentance means "I change." He also said that the repentance and water baptism he was ministering to his generation was to get them ready for Someone greater.

John says, "My water baptism is vastly inferior to His baptism." In other words, he said that what Jesus would do was so superior to his water baptism repentance, so much more powerful, that John was not worthy to even unloosen Jesus shoes. Yet, Jesus testifies that John was the greatest preacher of history to that time!

John says, "He will baptize you in Holy Spirit fire!" John illustrates or explains how this fire baptism operates. The picture is powerful!

THE FIRE THAT WILL NOT GO OUT

John is talking about the work of personal life-change repentance would release when Jesus baptizes with fire. That is, repentance sets us up for water baptism but the baptism of Jesus is a baptism of Holy Spirit fire. John uses a prophetic picture of the process harvested grain would go through to be useful and edible to illustrate this spiritual baptism.

> *He will baptize you in Holy Spirit and fire! His fan is in His hand. He will not stop until the entire floor is clean. He will burn the chaff in a fire that will not go out! [Matthew 3:11-12]*

In John's time, harvested grain would be piled on a threshing floor. On one side someone stood with a large leaf or fan with a long handle and would wave it up and down creating a consistent flow of air over the floor.

The piled grain would be thrown up into this current of air repeatedly. On the opposite side of the pile, the thresher would build a fire. The chaff loosened from the grain as it was repeatedly falling back down. And, at the same time, as it was thrown into the air, the loosened chaff would be blown by the wind into the fire.

Pile of grain the middle. Wind blowing on one side. Fire burning on the other side. Remember, John is describing the superior baptism of Jesus.

John says, "Jesus will create spiritual wind. He will separate and isolate everything in your life that needs to be destroyed. He will blow that into the fire."

Something is destroyed in redemption! Something is redeemed. The grain harvested would be separated from the chaff.

John says Jesus will never stop working the grain until He has completely cleansed His floor, until all the chaff is gone. All! This is the superior baptism of Jesus, the new spiritual condition of Holy Spirit and fire for every believer.

Jesus has no sympathy for anything that stands between you and your destiny. He will never stop until everything hindering you is destroyed!

He will keep working the grain, throwing it up again and again, blowing through the grain with spiritual wind, and separating the worthless chaff, until every piece of chaff is gone!

John says the fire never goes out! Jesus keeps working in my life, blowing chaff into that Holy Spirit fire. The spiritual wind keeps blowing through my life as His work isolates the chaff and blows it into the fire where it is destroyed.

Repentance surrenders the chaff to the wind of the Spirit. It is not part of my destiny. It must be destroyed to more fully redeem my life.

When Jesus Comes to Your House

When I was beginning school, my first grade teacher would read us a very good poem. I remember it still today. It read something like this:

"If Jesus came to your house

And knocked upon the door;

I'm sure you'd be more happy

Than you've ever been before."

It was a British child's poem and basically painted a picture of Jesus coming over for crumpets and tea. Quaint. Cute.

If Jesus came to your house, I'm sure you would want Him to sit in your best room, in your finest chair, and you would want Him to feel relaxed as you talked together. You would try to feed Him your best food and be the best example of the gift of hospitality the world has ever seen.

But when Jesus comes to your house, He won't sit in your finest chair. He won't relax in your best room. He hasn't come to take tea and taste your grandmother's best recipe for cookies. He has come to turn your world upside down, to offend your mind to show you what's in your heart, to open your eyes to the unseen motivations of your heart!

He will go the very closet you wish He'd never see, open the very drawer you wish He'd never open, and find the very things in your life you wish He'd ignore.

Because He is mean? No! God doesn't reveal your places of deepest pain, betrayal, wounding, sin, and deception to tease you, to tantalize you, to torment you. (That's the work of hell.) God's not coming to accuse you, but to set you free!

> *For God did not send the Son into the world to condemn it, but in order that, through Him, the world might be saved. [John 3:17]*

Jesus will go first to the places in your life that need cleansing. He will isolate the chaff in your life that needs to be blown into His consuming fire. He will never stop until everything that is hindering your destiny is destroyed in your life!

Remember, He will go after what is hindering the work of the Cross in your life.

Repentance is your surrender decision to release to the power of the Cross everything Jesus needs to destroy in your life that is keeping you from finding your life's work and destiny.

A Changed Heart

I remember the deep work God did in me. I was literally thrown to the floor, unable to move, as God sat on me and changed my life. I heard God say, "You are so proud and arrogant, filled with religion. Shut up. Stay still. I am doing surgery on you."

This was the beginning of my understanding of the spiritual roots God removes in redemption. Jesus always goes to the "heart of the matter." The heart must be changed as a first step to God's redemptive intervention.

The Old Testament sense of repentance is equally focused upon the heart issues. Joel quotes God as saying, "Turn to Me with all your heart." And, "Rend your hearts, not your clothing."

People in Joel's day would rip their clothing as if to expose their hearts to pain, grief, and repentance. They were doing a physical, prophetic action, but Joel says that action is not enough when it is but a show and not a reality.

We see repentance as "turning." Thinking one thing, repenting, because now I will think something else entirely different. Acting one way based upon previous mind-set, I am repenting because I have chosen a new, very different mind-set. Of course, repentance itself is my step toward the Cross. I change so God can change me. My decision in repentance opens my life to the power of the Cross.

David says, "Put Truth in my inward parts." Praying that the work of God would penetrate the dark places in his soul. This is a repentance prayer because repentance responds to revelation: "God show me what and where I need to change, and I will make the decision to open that area of my life to Your power."

God etched the Law upon stone tablets for Moses, but Jeremiah says the new covenant Jesus provides in the Cross would etch the words of God, what God wants in life and living, upon the hearts of His people.

Redemption is not simply recognition of what God wants, but the grace and spiritual power to do what God wants. This fulfills the law written on stone because its true intent is fulfilled in real life and living by those with Truth in their changed hearts.

> *One day, the Lord says, "I will make a new covenant with the houses of Israel and Judah: not like the covenant that I made with their fathers. I will put My law in their inward parts, and etch it upon their hearts." [Jeremiah 31:31-33]*

Repentance opens my heart for change. God changes my heart by the power of the Cross. I am different because God makes me different. Repentance and conversion operate together. They are both spiritual. They produce transformation inside that bears fruit outside. John the Baptist bridged the old covenant understanding of repentance into the new covenant work of Jesus.

Without the power of the Cross, repentance was simply a human attempt at change: "I change." But Jesus released spiritual power and authority into history that does more than mere human strength and wisdom: "I change to be changed." This is the new covenant Jesus Christ inaugurated and applies to humanity.

Jesus builds a new 'kingdom of God' message upon it. In fact, Jesus reveals this new repentance-based conversion as the entrance to that kingdom. Everything Jesus does and preaches is about life-change from the inside-out. He says, "There is now only one way to get into this spiritual kingdom, to live and function as a kingdom citizen, and to fulfill the purpose of kingdom in your life. You must change to be changed."

Truthfully, no one can get into God's kingdom unless he is born of water and spirit. Flesh births flesh, but spirit births spirit. The wind blows wherever it wants to. You hear the sound, but you cannot tell where it comes from or where it is going. So it is with everyone born of spirit." [John 3:5-8]

Out from the spirit inside, a new behavior and demonstration of life and living reveals itself outside. The newly-born spirit of man where the Spirit of God lives, operates, gifts, and manifests new life, new power, and new behavior. Repentance is the way to real, lasting transformation because all real, lasting change must begin in the spirit by the Spirit of God.

Spirit-First Living

When repentance opens my life to the work of Holy Spirit, He changes me inside-out. He sets spiritual conditions right in my heart so I can live "spirit-first."

In Level 2 of FreedomMinistry, we discuss SpiritFirst living in detail. Just as there is no substitute for the Cross (what we are discussing now in Level 1), there is no substitute for Holy Spirit (the essence of what we will discuss and experience in Level 2.)

Galatians 3 tells us that our life in Jesus Christ begins in spirit and must continue in spirit if we are to bring it to completion.

> *Starting by the Spirit, do you seriously think you can now reach fullness by your own human effort? [Galatians 3:3]*

Paul says, "How foolish you are to think that starting in the Spirit you would finish in the flesh! Did you receive Holy Spirit doing things in human wisdom and strength? Did you do miracles in human wisdom and strength? Then, why would think you could do what God wants outside the Spirit?" What God starts, God finishes. What starts spiritual continues Spirit-first.

God begins the repentance by revealing a new understanding. God waits only for my surrender decision to begin changing everything in my life and living inside-out by the work of Holy Spirit in me.

My repentance is more than a mental assent or acceptance of some religious idea. It is a spiritual response to a spiritual revelation.

Repentance begins a process of radical transformation of thought and will and feeling (everything in my soul) releasing me from sin and its power to control these areas of life and living, eventually bringing everything within me under the obedience and the will of God.

Receiving Prayer Ministry

Now, we will repeat prayers of repentance, renunciation, and declaration. We've gotta say somethin'!

And, as you exercise your will in speaking, the power of the Cross will be released within you to close the open doors. In repentance, you change to receive God's transforming grace.

You will come forward to receive prayer ministry from trained leaders. Your own words witness to your decision, and the prayer ministry seals those words and allows us to join in agreement with spiritual power and authority, laying hands on you to release the kingdom of God.

Jesus did it. Jesus taught His disciples to do it, and He said the Church would continue to do it until He returns.

So, receive this ministry of anointing prayer as Holy Spirit applies the power of the Cross to your life. You will experience the reality of what God is doing. You will be changed. You are choosing the power of the Cross, the Blood of Jesus, and the work of Holy Spirit.

It is powerful! Tens of thousands of others have received this breakthrough prayer ministry. So, speak with a strong voice without shouting or screaming, speak with conviction and faith, declare these prayers as we repent, renounce, rebuke, and receive.

4

The Gift of Forgiveness

Everything flows from the Cross. Jesus released the gift of forgiveness from the Cross. Jesus prayed, "Father, forgive them. They do not know what they do."

In that moment, Jesus surrendered His rights to justice, fairness, and judgment--while nailed to the Cross—and released a provision of forgiveness. He had the right to call for His Father to send an angelic army to set Him free, but He asked the Father to forgive His enemies. That is, Jesus had the right to justice but asked the Father to forgive instead.

That provision of forgiveness flows from the Cross into your life. Your sin pardon flows from the Cross! Your death pardon flows from the Cross. You are pardoned because Jesus is your substitute, and the Father is just to forgive your sins.

> *"If we confess our sins, He is faithful and just to forgive our sins and cleanse our unrighteousness." [I John 1:9]*

Jesus released the gift of forgiveness from the Cross as a provision for every sin for every man for all time; so, a provision of forgiveness is now available for everything you have done and everything that has been done to you. The Father is just to forgive you and give you a gift to forgive your enemies.

So, through the forgiveness of Jesus and what He did on the Cross, you can be forgiven and receive a provision of forgiveness for those who have wronged you.

Jesus asked Father to forgive His enemies. He surrendered His right to justice and fairness. He had the right to judgment. He had the right to call His Father's angel army to destroy them. He had the right to fairness for this unspeakable atrocity. He asked for pardon instead.

You are forgiven, and you can forgive. The grace of the Cross that forgives your sins also makes the grace available for you to forgive others. That is why Jesus charges you to forgive others as Father has forgiven you. The grace gift of forgiveness comes to you from the Father by the power of the Cross!

"FATHER FORGIVE"

Notice Jesus asks the Father to forgive. He prays, "Father, forgive them." The grace gift that forgives you comes from the Father. The grace that you need to forgive others comes from the Father too!

> *For the Father rescued us from the domain of darkness, and transferred us into the kingdom of His beloved Son, in whom we have redemption, the forgiveness of sins. [Colossians 1:13-14]*

Father saved, transferred, redeemed, and forgave you through Jesus Christ, His Son. The Father is the One who forgives. He can do that and be a just and holy God because Jesus took your sins upon Himself. Jesus Christ met the demands of justice and fairness against you for what you have done, and the demands of justice and fairness for what "they" did to you.

When Jesus asks Father to forgive, Jesus is releasing His rights to justice, fairness, and judgment. He is being wronged—wronged in the ultimate sense. The injustice against Jesus is greater than any injustice, piling up the greatest demand for judgment possible. Yet, Jesus says, "Father, I release my rights to judgment."

In doing so, Jesus further completes His work on the Cross and releases the greatest forgiveness possible. His work makes it just for Father to forgive every man for every sin! Jesus releases the gift or provision of forgiveness for you to forgive every man for every wrong against you. You are asking Father God to forgive those who have done you wrong.

The same grace that forgives you gives you the capacity to forgive others. You choose to release that forgiveness by receiving something from the Father and releasing to those who have wronged you. This is a spiritual provision, not something you develop or earn on your own, not your wisdom in figuring out the situations, or your strength to deal with your issues.

The Cross is your source and resource for forgiveness. Jesus released the provision for forgiveness there.

You don't possess the ultimate power or authority to forgive others. Father does. All sin is ultimately sin against the Father and requires an accounting with God. Jesus did something on the Cross that gives Him authority to deal with God for us, authority to pardon.

When you forgive others, you receive grace from the Father to pardon them for what they have done. Father will deal with them about how they have wronged Him.

Loved ones, never take your own revenge, exacting your own punishment, but allow for God's punishment, for it is written, "Vengeance is Mine. I will repay," says the Lord. [Romans 12:19]

Leave the righting of wrongs to God. Taking on the role God has kept for Himself sets you up for unresolved anger, grief, and bitterness. These conditions will seep poison into every part of your life because they are open doors to the work of hell, and hell will use them to develop systems of bitter resentment.

When you confess your own sins and He forgives, He also makes a grace gift available that gives you the capacity to forgive others. You receive it from Him and release your rights to justice, fairness, and judgment. The gift operates when you make a decision to forgive others who have wronged you.

To understand the forgiveness the Cross provides, you must first see that all wrongs are ultimately against God, that you give accounting to Him ultimately for what you have done and what has been done to you. God has to make the decision about these wrongs to hand down judgment.

What you do requires His judgment. What people do to you requires His judgment. What hell does to you requires His judgment. "Judgment" is God's decision on the matter.

In the Cross, Jesus took the judgment upon Himself for what you did, what people did to you, and what hell has done to steal, kill, and destroy your destiny. His death fulfills the covenant or agreement God made to redeem a fallen world. So, in Jesus, the Father can determine the judgment of every person.

This means that forgiveness is possible because the sins to be forgiven were judged in the Cross. In other words, because of what Jesus did on the Cross, the Father can deal with every person, every situation, and every issue. He can forgive. He can punish. Because of the Cross, it is all in Father's hands.

So, all forgiveness comes by the Cross from the Father. Jesus prays on the Cross, "Father forgive them."

They Don't Know

Jesus prays, "Forgive them, for they don't know what they

do." They are aware of their actions. They are consciously deciding to do what they are doing. They are really doing the wrong that needs to be forgiven. However, they cannot know the actual consequences of what they are doing.

Forgiveness is never simply ignoring or forgetting what really occurred. Merely avoiding the issues that have damaged our lives, ignoring them, or denying they happened can never release true forgiveness to those who wronged us or release us from the power of those wrongs. Forgiveness is never denial.

"They don't know what they do" isn't about denial or forgetting what really happened. They did know what they were doing when they were crucifying Jesus. They even said, "Let His blood be upon our heads." They shouted, "Crucify!" They spat and cursed. They shouted and raved.

However, they could never know what they were really doing, the consequences of the deeds they had chosen to perform. This is a principle of forgiveness: you forgive those who did you wrong although they never experience the pain and suffering their actions have caused.

Your abusers knew they were abusing you, but they didn't know the nights you would be awake with terror, the wounding of your soul and the dysfunctional relationships of your wounded life, or the agony you feel abusing others from the out-of-control behaviors their abuse planted in your soul.

The business partner that stole from you and destroyed your company knew he was stealing, but he didn't know the days you would suffer, unable to meet your family's needs or give your loved ones what you wanted to give them. They didn't know the doubt and fear you harbor from days of dread and insecurity. They didn't know that you now find it impossible to trust anyone because of their betrayal.

People who have wronged you knew what they were choosing to do even when their behaviors were out of control, but they could never fully know the spiritual and eternal consequences of their actions.

They were unaware of the hidden response of your heart to the words they spoke, the looks they gave, the actions they took. They were blind, selfish, driven by demanding lusts, pain, greed, and witchcraft. They don't know how it feels. They didn't know the sleepless nights, the agony of regret, the pain of depression, or the despair that crushed your ambitions. And, they don't know that their actions placed them under eternal judgment, but neither did you when you wronged others yourself.

Forgetting is not enough and usually not really possible. Rewriting history is only a form of avoidance behavior and mental illness. Leaving issues of offense to time is a mistake. The shadows of those events remain in place speaking into the way you respond to life today. Time heals nothing!

Forgiveness recognizes the real pain and suffering others have caused and the eternal judgment against them, and chooses to receive forgiveness from the Father and release full pardon to them anyway. Forgiveness isn't finding a way to excuse their actions, blame yourself, or balance the score because you feel that you have failed somehow as well as they did.

Some of the issues of forgiveness can only be known when Holy Spirit brings them to the surface. Dealing with them on our own can sometimes be too painful because we buried them long ago to protect ourselves from the pain. Holy Spirit brings them to the surface so we can take them to the Cross!

Forgiveness Flows from the Cross

When you forgive, you release yourself, free yourself, as you release the ones who have wronged you. Unforgiveness is spiritual bondage. It leads to bitterness, the poison of the soul and spirit. It is a root that produces many other fruits. It poisons other people with its pain.

One woman said, "I hate doctors. My mother would be alive now if her doctor hadn't failed her. He messed up the surgery, and she died."

A rape victim said, "I hate men. I was raped by one. They are all the same."

A middle-aged man said, "I was abused by my uncle. Now, I abuse others. He did this to me. I am what I am because of what he did."

Divorce sets people up for unforgiveness. Men, women, children suffer from the pain, betrayal, and loneliness of divorce. The bitterness surfaces in later relationships because of unforgiveness.

Forgiveness releases you from wrongs done to you and is often the key to unlocking out-of-control behaviors. Other root issues remain fully functional within you when you are unwilling to forgive. Physical and mental suffering are sometimes sourced in your secret place of blame.

Forgiveness Cancels Judgment

Whenever you participate in judgment, you are judged by the same judgment. Forgiveness cancels out the judgment due and releases you from the same judgment on your own life. In this way, forgiveness sets you free.

There is a difference between judgment and reaping what you have sown. In each case, mercy can release you from the consequences of your failures and sins, but judgment is more about punishment than harvest. Judgment is more about ultimate terms of destruction; reaping is more about learning from our experiences.

Jesus ties forgiveness to forgiving. He charges you to forgive because the Father cannot forgive you when you are unwilling to forgive. There is a direct connection between unforgiveness and condemnation.

You are tied to your enemies when you fail to forgive them. You reap what they sow in you because you make it your own, feed it, protect it, and act upon it until it defines who you are. You become like the people you refuse to forgive.

This is part of the reason why abused people become abusers, why those who suffered with alcoholic parents become alcoholics. They are bound to damaging behaviors that hurt them because they demand their rights to justice and judgment. They receive the same judgment themselves. Unforgiveness is a fetter, a chain, and a jail cell, which binds and imprisons you with the person who wronged you.

Bitterness

When you harbor unforgiveness, you are carrying bitterness in your soul, a poison that causes you to look at other people through the spiritual filter of your unresolved pain. This burden of unforgiveness cripples you. At some level, you cannot fully receive physical and emotional healing. It affects your prayer life, your worship, your ministry, your marriage, your relationships, and your mind.

Unforgiven wrong remains an open door to the work of hell; only the Father can close that door in the power of the Cross.

If you are refusing to take this issue to the Cross, you have chosen to deal with it in your own wisdom and strength. You suffer the consequences—an open door allows hell to work in your heart. At some point, it is not only the wrong done to you at work, but hell operating through unforgiveness, working bitterness into your heart. The wrong done to you has "taken on a life of its own" in the spirit, energized by demonic strategy.

But if you do not forgive others, then your Father will not forgive your transgressions. [Matthew 6:15]

Unforgiveness means Father cannot do a work of forgiveness in your life that would cancel this claim of hell.

You justify your retributive attitude, replaying events, exaggerating them to justify your response of unforgiveness. You relive it, refreshing the pictures and images of your feelings and thoughts, holding mini-arguments like a courtroom within yourself.

You express yourself in repeated rehearsals of what was done to you. You express anger and disappointment disproportionate to the present situations you are dealing with because you are still living in the shadows of that history. You also discover a hidden satisfaction about anything negative that seems to hit their lives.

You have a behavioral pattern of melodrama. Your reactions to people and situations don't seem to fit the facts. Seemingly insignificant things overly upset you. You are bound by over-reaction that is a swirling whirlpool of drama.

You may project the pain of your past upon people with whom you have relationship or contact today. Bitterness targets men because a man hurt you. The bitterness attaches to doctors because a doctor hurt you. The bitterness focuses upon pastors because a pastor hurt you.

Of course, painful memories may cause you to avoid things that remind you of your suffering. This is understandable but unnecessary. This is different from bitterness.

Bitterness is an operation of spiritual darkness within the soul and poisons your personality. Self-pity flows from bitterness, along with cynicism, judgment, curse, and negativity.

Do you wonder why you react to some people and some forms of input with such violent over-reaction and confusion? Do you realize the power of past pain when you put people into categories: "You are just like my mother. You are just like that pastor we had when I was young. You are just like ..." These are symptoms of bitterness.

As long as you hold on to your right to fairness and justice, you cannot receive the pardon that sets you free in this area of your life, and you continue to suffer the consequences of the wrong someone else did to you. You want the person who did you wrong to suffer for it, "to get what they deserve."

Because you are the one injured, you must be the one to release the judgment against the other person; but until you do, you will suffer the same judgment and become just like them.

This is "bitter root judgment." It is a spiritual poison. It is your decision to value vengeance more than freedom. Because you don't forgive, you are not forgiven. The very spiritual condition that is motivating their wrongs against you begins to operate in your own heart.

You become like the people you don't forgive.

The Root of Bitterness

Unforgiveness is an open door, and hell will use this open door to spread poison to other areas of your life.

> *See to it that no one fails to obtain the grace of God and that no bitter root grows up and causes you trouble, or many of you will become defiled. [Hebrews 12:15]*

This Scripture refers to Esau, the older brother of Jacob. He was the firstborn but gave up his birthright for a bowl of stew because he held his inheritance in contempt. Later, he was filled with regret. He was always an aggressive, unforgiving, and bitter person after that because a root of bitterness grew in his soul.

The conflict between the families of Esau and Israel continues to this day as if Esau is still demanding the destruction of his brother with no sense of forgiveness.

Bitterness will put down roots. It will grow. It will produce bitter fruit. It will spread and defile others. When you judge or refuse to give up your right to judgment, you are judged. A root of judgment inside of you grows up. There is no healing or restoration in this judgment, because this judgment demands punishment, "getting what is deserved."

When you judge others, you are saying, "Don't allow them to be restored." This judgment judges you, and you remain stuck in bondage. Because of unforgiveness, you are not restored from the damage of your enemies' wrongs! Your unforgiveness becomes a prison.

Jesus says unlimited forgiveness is the norm of the kingdom of God. While telling a story of a man forgiven of much—what would be equivalent to the national debt—Jesus reveals the spiritual significance of unforgiveness.Forgiven of an insurmountable debt, the forgiven man hurries from the presence of the king who forgave him and puts a man in jail for owing him the cost of a Happy Meal.

Hearing of this, the king puts the previously pardoned man in jail until he repays all he owes—forever—he did not forgive others for little wrongs when he was forgiven a debt impossible to repay.

> *My heavenly Father will also do the same to you, if each of you does not forgive his brother from your heart. [Matthew 18:35]*

Forgiveness is a heart issue. It will produce behaviors that spring up and trouble every part of your life. You are locked away, in debt to God for your own sins, because you will not receive and release the gift of forgiveness to others.

An Advantage for Satan

Paul says, this is a strategy or method of hell to create more misunderstanding, division, and mischief in the Body of Christ, and we are not ignorant of his ways. Paul says, "We don't want to give satan an opening to work in the Body."

> *When you forgive anything, I forgive also; for whatever I have forgiven, I forgive in Christ's presence to help you, so satan has no advantage over us, for we have experience with the way he works. [2 Corinthians 2:10-11]*

This Scripture refers specifically to forgiveness because unforgiveness gives hell an advantage over us. It is an open door. Through that open door, hell will build a structure of bitterness. The unforgiveness will "take on a life of its own."

This reference reminds us of our teaching on "Closing Open Doors:" Don't give the devil an opportunity. Paul says unforgiveness is an open door. Until the man he mentions in this passage knows he is forgiven, he remains separated from the life-giving relationships of the Church, and hell establishes a breech in the Body, the very opposite of what Paul set out to accomplish in this situation.

GET FREE! FORGIVE!

The moment you receive and release the gift of forgiveness, you will be set up for freedom. When you release them, you release yourself. You say, "They hurt me. They did me wrong. I need justice!" No, you need healing and restoration. That healing and restoration comes from the Cross.

You say, "But you don't know what they did to me!" No, and I don't need to know because whatever they have done can be forgiven. God would forgive them because of the Cross, and you can forgive them when you receive and release the provision of forgiveness that comes from the Cross.

No, I don't know what they did to you, but you are still suffering from it and bringing greater suffering to your life and the lives of others because you won't forgive them. The damage of your unforgiveness is worse than the damage of what they did to you.

Here's the judgment you think they deserve: they deserve what they did to you or worse to happen to them, so you want to do to them what they did to you. You want them to get what they deserve. That means you are just like them. You have become like the people you won't forgive.

You need to let it go! You must make a surrender decision. You need to release them from judgment. You can pray, "Father, forgive them. I don't want them to receive judgment for what they did." You ask the Father for the provision of forgiveness and you pray for your enemies. You set them free so you can be free.

Dealing with Offense

God has a particular way of dealing with offense. The offense is a work of darkness we receive when someone does us wrong. It is a strategy of hell, a trap set through this wrong; the offense is more than someone doing us wrong.

Offense means to put something in someone's path that will ensnare him or her if they fall into it or step into it. Offense is a trap set by hell to ensnare us, and we can only fall into offense by stepping into the trap.

Offense comes more easily to us when we are shallow in our understanding. Jesus spoke of offense in these terms while teaching about how the word of God is received. Shallow understanding leaves more open to offense.

> *Because he has no root, he endures for a while but when tribulation or persecution comes because of the word, he is offended. [Matthew 13:21]*

Shallow understanding or commitment to the word will produce a sense of entitlement that withers in the heat of the day. We are offended when the word demands change, and one of the startling changes people face with Jesus is the expectation of forgiving their enemies.

So, we must deal with offense by the power of the Cross, receiving Christ's redemptive provision to get out of hell's entrapment. Offense involves forgiveness, but offense is more than someone doing us wrong. Offense is a work of darkness that takes on a life of its own.

The solution to offense is deeper than avoiding the person offending us, forgetting the incident, or running away from the situation. The solution involves both the person doing us wrong, and the trap into which we fell because of their doing us wrong.

Technically speaking, someone does not offend us as much as he or she do us wrong and we fall into offense because of the wrong done to us. Forgiveness is the first step, but offense must be broken by the power of the Cross. We must receive the Cross' power to release us from the trap.

Once offended, the offense produces a spiritual death cycle of its own that can follow us around for decades. Running from the offense or failing to take that offense to the Cross leaves us open to more and more offense, isolation, bitterness, and a persecution complex. We learn to blame everyone else for our unhappiness.

In other words, once offense captures us, we become a person more vulnerable to offense. When others do us wrong, as will happen in the course of life, we fall into more traps and develop an offended soul.

When we fall into an offense trap, fail to take it to the Cross, leave that situation bitter, we will carry that offense into future situations, relationships, and experiences. The offense becomes bigger than one person's wrong.

If we leave a difficult situation without proper resolution, we will carry the offense until the power of the Cross breaks us free. Many years may pass before we see the offense we have hidden in our heart. We will realize it is no longer about the wrong someone did to us, but something bigger is influencing our souls.

Many Christians wander from church to church with offenses because they fail to receive the gift of forgiveness and take their offenses to the Cross. They become vagabonds.

Receiving Prayer Ministry

Now, we will repeat prayers of repentance, renunciation, and declaration. We've gotta say somethin'! And, as you exercise your will in speaking, the power of the Cross will be released. In repentance, you change to be changed.

You will receive the gift of forgiveness from the Father and release it to those He has revealed need that forgiveness. You will receive release the chains of unforgiveness!

You will come forward to receive prayer ministry from trained leaders. Your own words witness to your decision, and the prayer ministry seals those words and allows us to join in agreement with spiritual power and authority, laying hands on you to release the kingdom of God.

Jesus did it. Jesus taught His disciples to do it, and He said the Church would continue to do it until He returns. So, receive this ministry of anointing prayer as Holy Spirit applies the power of the Cross to your life. You will be changed. You are choosing the power of the Cross, the Blood of Jesus, and the work of Holy Spirit.

It is powerful! Tens of thousands of others have received this breakthrough prayer ministry. So, speak with a strong voice without shouting or screaming, speak with conviction and faith, declare these prayers as we repent, renounce, rebuke and receive.

5

The Cleansing Walk

FreedomMinistry is not only about getting free, but learning spiritual skills you need to walk in that freedom, staying free for the rest of your life. The battle for freedom continues, and you must be vigilant, aggressive, and faithful to both keep your freedom and expand that freedom.

Walking means living. The New Testament describes the Christian life as "the Way" and uses the action of walking to discuss living the life of Jesus in mortal flesh. Walking is a step by step, daily walk with the Father.

> *As we walk in the light as Father is in the light, we have fellowship with one another, and the blood of Jesus Christ, His Son, cleanses us from all sin. [1 John 1:7]*

The Father is Light. Living in His light with Him, is a spiritual fellowship, one with the other. Within this relationship, light reveals us openly and truly and we receive a cleansing stream washing what is revealed of sin from our lives.

You might first interpret this as walking in the Father's light as Jesus is walking in His light, sharing with Jesus in the Father's light a consistent flow of redemptive grace which the blood of God's Son provides that cleans your life from sin.

It is a lifestyle of walking out purity of soul, a step-by-step process of restoring fully what Father desired your life to be so you can do all He has called you to do. The cleansing power of the blood of Jesus continues working within you in this life of fellowship with Father.

The Stain is Not Too Deep!

It does not matter what you have done, what's been done to you, or what hell is doing in your life right now, the Blood of Jesus can cleanse the stain from your life!

You say, "The stain's too deep!"

He says, "My Blood's gone deeper."

You say, "I've gone too far!"

He says, "My Blood's gone farther."

You say, "I've done too much!"

He says, "My Blood's done more."

The Blood cleanses it. The grace of God surpasses it. The end result is you have victory over it.

God does not flinch when He deals with your worst issues. While some wounds or evils are too gruesome and dreadful for us to contemplate, God has seen it all a billion times, and longs to set you free through the cleansing power of the Blood!

Consider this: God already knew what you did, what others did to you, and what hell has been doing in your life before He called you to life, inheritance, and walking with Him. Father knows the power of the Cross, so He wants to apply that power to break, remove, and cleanse your life, inside-out.

He knows where to start, what to do next, and how quickly you can stand the process. Because He is not only forgiving and cleansing but also restoring, He walks you into the transformation. He gets involved, remains involved to the end. Father keeps uncovering hidden areas of spiritual darkness and removing them.

The Cleansing Walk

"Walking" means "behavior, lifestyle, and habits." Walking speaks of how you live your life. "Walking in the light" means living in the light. It means living out what the power of the Cross has worked in.

Walking in the light as Father is in the light means that His Presence illuminates our lifestyle and behavior. He is in the details of our lives, living with us, walking us into understanding and revelation of His ways and our ways revealed by His Light.

Once we begin this process of surrendering to the power of the Cross, Father gets deeply involved in our lives to release the power of the Cross to cleanse us from all sin.

> *As we walk in the light as He is in the light, we have fellowship with one another. [1 John 1:7]*

Father is walking with us. Fellowship means that He takes a part of the responsibility for our behavior, to get involved in revealing what that behavior is and the roots of that lifestyle. Father reveals our motivations.

Light reveals. Paul tells us in Ephesians that light is what manifests or reveals, that we should "walk as children of light." That follows closely what John is saying in this Scripture. Children walking with Father. He is Light, and we walk in light when we walk with Him. Light reveals.

Father's light does not reveal us to tease, torment, or tantalize us. He reveals us to cleanse us, change us, and consecrate us. Father walks with us to apply the blood of Jesus, the power of the Cross, to our lives.

FATHER'S FELLOWSHIP

Father sent Jesus to die for you so He could walk with you. He desires you, desires your company, and desires your fellowship. In this walking companionship with Father, He is applying the power of the Cross to your life and living to not only forgive your sins but to break the controlling power and influence of sin in your life.

> *We have fellowship with one another, and the blood of Jesus Christ, His Son, cleanses us from all sin. [1 John 1:7]*

We enter that fellowship through the Cross and the Cross continues operating in our lives as we walk in fellowship with God. The power of the Cross to cleanse sin continues working in our lives until the Light reveals all and the Blood cleanses all. Father will never quit until that work of cleansing is completed - "cleanses us from all sin."

As we have learned in Section 2, "Closing Open Doors," Jesus has the right to break every claim of hell to operate within us. His Cross was a perfect sacrifice, offering pure Blood, a Perfect Man taking our place, the complete and perfect Substitute, to redeem us, buy us back from hell's control and influence.

Sin opens doors. Cleansing away sin gives us the opportunity to close those doors. "Walking with the Father" naturally opens our lives to His Light and the Blood cleanses us from all sin. Step by step, so to speak, as we walk with Father, more cleansing occurs.

Fellowship is a very special Bible word. Although the concept has been colored by mundane uses, the Biblical sense of fellowship is more than a social relationship, a mutual "let's just get along as friends and have a good time" sort of picture. Fellowship is a covenant word every time it is used in Scripture.

Covenant means that you take a part with God, and God takes a part with you. This sounds like share and share alike, but it is much, much more. It is commitment, consecration, and covenant.

Fellowship means that you make a commitment to what Father is doing, and Father makes a commitment to what you are doing. That's the sense of the word "walk" in this context. Walk is behavior and lifestyle. So, fellowship means that you involve yourself in what Father is doing and Father involves Himself in what you are doing.

Of course, this is all massively to your benefit since involving yourself with what Father is doing opens your life to God, and what Father is doing is an eternal work of redemption!

THE CLEANSING POWER OF THE BLOOD

The power of the Blood is the power of the Cross upon which the Blood of Christ was shed. At the Cross, Jesus' Blood was released to fulfill a Divine Plan that included substitution.

Someone could take the place of someone else. Death was required for the penalty of sin, and Jesus' death substitutes for you. The Blood of Jesus not only removes the need for death, it also has the power to break the demands of sin against you.

> *According to Moses' law, nearly everything was cleansed by sprinkled blood, and without bloodshed, no*

sins are forgiven. That is why the earthly worship tent and everything in it (heavenly replicas) required cleansing with blood, but the heavenly worship they represent required cleansing with a far better sacrifice than animal blood.

For Christ has entered into heaven itself as our Intercessory representative before God; that's why He didn't enter the earthly worship tent, for that was merely a copy of the real worship in heaven, nor did He set up a system to enter heaven to offer himself repeatedly. He came once, ultimately, and finally removing sin's power by His substitutionary, sacrificial death. [Hebrews 9:21-26]

Sin cannot control or influence your behavior when it has been removed as a motivating influence in our heart. The Blood cleanses away both the stain of sins you have committed, and the condition of sin in your heart motivating your life.

The power of the Blood is the power of the Cross! The Blood of Jesus has power to remove spiritual conditions within your soul that are sources of sinful behaviors. Since deception is a basic characteristic of sin's strategy, the Light exposes the hidden systems of sinfulness so the cleansing power of Christ's Blood can remove them.

Notice the indisputable boldness of the Scripture to declare the power of the Blood to cleanse all sin. Without hesitation, John says, "All." All kinds of sin? (I John 1:7) Yes. All that sin has established in my life? Yes. Every sin I have committed, leaving its mark on my mind, emotions, and decisions? Yes.

He gave His life to set us free from every aspect and behavior of sin, to cleanse us, and to make us His very own people, sold out to doing what is right. [Titus 2:14]

It is the goal of Father to bring everything sin is and does in your life to the Light, expose it to the power of the Blood, to cleanse and remove it from you!

Keep Walking

Your cleansing has begun. It is not finished until all sin is cleansed. Father is walking with you because He wants you, but the cleansing keeps happening as long as you walk in the Light.

In other words, Father is not walking with you only to cleanse you, merely to apply the Blood of His Son to you. No. He is walking with you because you have begun the cleansing and are ready for fellowship with Him. He wants to fellowship with you, and can only walk with you because of the Blood of Jesus.

In FreedomMinistry, we have drawn from the best materials, experiences, and teachings of several generations of discipling leadership. We have done more than bring cleansing to your life. We have taught you how to appropriate the power of the Cross for cleansing and given you spiritual skills so you can stay free, and walk with Father in deeper cleansing.

Because we have a great High Priest ruling from the heavenlies, so let's go right on in with boldness in our hearts, sprinkled with Christ's blood to cleanse us inside, and washed with pure water outside. (Compare Hebrews 4:16 and 10:22)

So, keep walking! Expect cleansing! You will see the need for deeper cleansing as you walk in the Light with Father, and your repentance, renouncing, and rebuking of sinful sources of behavior will continue to be removed from your life and living.

You may make some more bad choices, and you may sin again. FreedomMinistry does not remove the possibility of sin, but establishes spiritual skills to confess, repent, renounce, and break the power of any sin and sinful practice in your life.

Everything flows to you from the Cross. When the Father's Light reveals, the Son's Blood cleanses. You see, the Father knows that the Blood is your source and resource for removing sin from your life. The Blood of His Son.

Do not fall into the deception that once you have experienced some cleansing, you do not need more cleansing. Keep in fellowship with Father. The Blood of His Son will not fail to meet you at the point of repentance, for when you have a heart for God, to be clean before Him, all sin revealed by the Light calls you to the power of the Cross.

In some ways, beginning in cleansing reveals the greater need for cleansing. It is like the adage about learning: "the more I know, the more I realize how little I know." The more I am cleansed, the more I realize how I need more cleansing.

Do not think that FreedomMinistry is a "once and for all" magic wand. There is no magic wand. There is a redemptive walk.

Keep walking in the Light! Father knows where and when to shine His Light. For you to go to the places of your deep darkness without Him can bring despair instead of change. The Light is so bright and the darkness so dark, that you must go to that place of cleansing in your life with Him, with the power of the Cross, with the revelation of repentance.

Father knows how to restore you and rebuild your identity. He first thought of you and Jesus created you because Father wants you. Father is restoring you to the person He wanted. No one knows you like God does!

Scripture is full of admonition, or advice charged with the demand for commitment. "Get clean. Stay clean." Get free! Stay free!

Do not think that hell will simply let you go without a fight. No. The battle is just beginning. You must learn to fight with the power of the Cross, in the power of the Spirit.

The Stronger One

Jesus talks about this spiritual process in reference to displacing demon spirits from people during His ministry. His words are revelation about how things operate in the spirit, and about what breaking the controlling influences of demonic spirits does in your life.

There is a controlling spiritual influence in your life. This is true of every person. The extent to which that spiritual influence controls a person's behavior is dynamic and depends upon the decisions that person makes.

> *No man can serve two masters: either he will hate one and despise the other, or he will hold one and despise the other. You cannot serve God and riches. [Matthew 6:24]*

Jesus assumes that spiritual influences are controlling some aspects of your thinking and behavior. Spiritual influences operate in your heart, and your heart is not physical but spiritual.

Some of these influences are your own since you act upon what you believe, what you desire, what you love; you act upon motivations of your heart. Some of these influences are from hell when hell is operating through open doors to your soul building strongholds or systems of spiritual influence within you or hell is operating from the outside to gain influence and control.

> *If I am casting out demons by God's Spirit, then God's Kingdom has arrived. You can't enter a strong man's house and rob him without first incapacitating him. Only then can his house be robbed! [Matthew 12:28-29]*

Jesus describes the controlling influences captured by hell as "a strong man" who has taken possession of a house. While this is the sense in which the erroneous concept of "demon possession" arises, the truth is that hell has taken possession of some aspects of your heart.

When the stronger man comes, he takes away the weapons of the strong man, kicks him out of the house he has stolen, and brings the house under his own control.

Jesus says all this in the context of discussing the kingdom of hell and the kingdom of heaven. The strong man represents the influence and control of hell. The stronger man is Jesus Himself, greater and more powerful than any claim of hell on any house!

Every person has hellish influences operating within them until those controlling influences are broken, removed, and overcome by the power of the Cross. You are a child of disobedience before you are changed through repentance. You are operating by the spirit of this world, the spirit of mammon, the spirit of religion, the spirit of deception, for example, spiritual conditions of spiritual influence that control certain aspects of your behavior, thinking, and decisions.

As you become a Christian, the cleansing walk begins. You walk as children of light, walking in the Light with Father, and you walk into confrontations that demand cleansing.

> *For once you were darkness, but now you are light in the Lord. Live as children of light, for the behavior of the light produces all goodness, righteousness and truth.*
>
> *As well, discover what pleases the Lord. Have nothing to do with the darkness and deadly behaviors. Rather, expose them. For to even mention the covert behavior of the disobedient is shameful.*
>
> *However, light exposes everything, making it obvious. For light reveals everything. [Ephesians 5:8-14]*

Walking in light becomes the basis and motivation of behavior that produces good, righteous, real actions, and also reveals what pleases God. Ignore the operations of darkness as a source motivation for your behavior because everything will become obvious, shown for what it really is.

When the Light reveals the need for cleansing, repent. Let God's light show you what needs cleansing. Change to be changed! Repentance appropriates the power of the Cross. When you see pride operating in your life, repent of pride. The behaviors of pride will be weakened by the removal of the motivations of your heart. Begin inside to change behavior outside.

While that sounds easy, it is a battle! Depending upon your own strength will not bring freedom. Surrender to the power of the Cross.

Fill the House

Jesus says that the spiritual strong man who has been evicted from the house will go and seek help from other spirits worse than he is. He will attempt to take back what he has lost.

The battle will not be over when the stronger man evicts the work of hell. The battle will begin in a greater measure. Hell is looking for an empty house, a vulnerable house.

> *When an unclean spirit departs a man, it goes through dry places looking for a place to stop its wandering. When it does not find a place, it says, 'I will return to the house I left.' When it gets there, it finds the house swept clean and spruced up. Then it creates an alliance with seven more oppressive spirits, and they go in and live there. The man's resulting state of affairs is worse than the first. [Luke 11:20-26]*

Being set free is a new beginning, but the confrontation and defeat of the influences and control of hell is not over. The strategy of hell to reestablish a door of opportunity to operate within you continues, and the work of hell will continue against you from the outside.

The vicious cycle of temptation will continue hammering the same areas of weakness and vulnerability that gave hell entrance to your soul in the past. Knowing your weakness, hell will continue to seek for an opportunity. Be aware. Be on guard.

> *Do not be intoxicated with wine, for that brings ruin. In contrast, maintain the fullness of being under the influence of Holy Spirit. [Ephesians 5:18]*

You must fill the house, your life - spirit, soul, and body - with Holy Spirit. You are God's temple, a house for His Spirit to live within you. There is no substitute for the power of the Cross, and there is no substitute for the power of Holy Spirit!

Receiving Prayer Ministry

Now, we will repeat prayers of repentance, renunciation, and declaration. We've gotta say somethin'!

And, as you exercise your will in speaking, the power of the Cross will be released. In repentance, you change to be changed.

You have learned how to receive cleansing and transformation. You will take these skills with you as you continue walking in cleansing and transformation.

You will come forward to receive prayer ministry from trained leaders. Your own words witness to your decision, and the prayer ministry seals those words and allows us to join in agreement with spiritual power and authority, laying hands on you to release the kingdom of God.

Jesus did it. Jesus taught His disciples to do it, and He said the Church would continue to do it until He returns.

So, receive this ministry of anointing prayer as Holy Spirit applies the power of the Cross to your life. You will experience the reality of what God is doing. You will be changed. You are choosing the power of the Cross, the Blood of Jesus, and the work of Holy Spirit.

It is powerful! Tens of thousands of others have received this breakthrough prayer ministry. So, speak with a strong voice without shouting or screaming, speak with conviction and faith, declare these prayers as we repent, renounce, rebuke and receive.

www.ingramcontent.com/pod-product-compliance
Lightning Source LLC
Chambersburg PA
CBHW071826020426
42331CB00007B/1624
9780692266045